The Call

By: Robert E. Savage, Sr.

Acknowledgements

I would like to thank my wife, Jennifer, and our children for their support and encouragement during the process of writing this book. Without their support, this project would have never taken shape. I would also like to thank Pastor Barbara Cannon and the members of His Freedom Reigns Ministries for their encouraging prayers and support during my transformation.

I would also like to thank Mark and Ana Shelley for their unwavering friendship and support through this educational process. Their friendship helped me keep reaching. I would also like to thank Lt. Christy Nebel for proof reading and editing this manuscript, a challenge for any English major.

I would also like to thank Chief Russell Abernathy for his spiritual leadership, and his Christian walk in life that is apparent to all. I would also like to thank Major Stoney Mathis for his sincere support, not only in the work place, but also in the spiritual realm. Without this support, and direction, this project might not have been published.

And I would like to thank Reverend Ralph Easterwood of the Glen Haven Baptist Church who gave so willingly of himself during our conversations that pushed for the publication of this manuscript. I thank you for the support and encouragement.

And lastly, I would like to thank the Lord Jesus Christ for equipping and helping me accomplish such a feat. The joy that He has provided in my life is indescribable. The mercy that He has shown me I have not deserved. I thank you for all that you have done for me. Let Your will be done!

Dedication Page

This book is dedicated to "my bride" Jennifer, to whom I will always be thankful!

Table of Contents

Forward

Ith is rare to hear from law enforcement on significant keys to spiritual insights of God's Kingdom. In this book Robert Savage combines the two: Law Enforcement and God's Kingdom. He is a man who has served his community through Law Enforcement for 19 years. A man, who understands the authority of the law and has enforced this authority to protect the citizens of our city.

I am honored to write this forward because I have seen God transform this man's life before my very eyes. A man who has seen and went through many trials pertaining to life and living, now sharing with us the experience he has with the Lord.

As the Pastor of His Freedom Reigns Ministries, I know that the authority of Law Enforcement and the authority of God's Kingdom are parallel in many ways. God has called Robert Savage to minister for Him in truth of the Lord Jesus Christ and to use the authority on the name of Jesus to bind evil and to spread the good news that Jesus saves, heals, and delivers.

I know as Robert has fought crime in our community, this man of God is now fighting crime in God's Kingdom. As he has answered the call of God in his life to share Jesus and to be an example to us that God is still changing lives, I believe that your life will be changed as you receive the message that Robert Savage has written in this book.

May the Lord bless you as you read THE CALL!

Pastor Barbara Cannon
President/Founder
His Freedom Reigns Ministries

<u>Introduction</u>

The Call

As I was preparing this book, I decided that as a first time author that I owed it to the reading public to provide some background information on myself, to qualify in some degree the validity of this publication.

I am a nineteen-year veteran law enforcement officer, working in Georgia, for the Henry County Police Department. My wife and I have six children, and are devout Christians. We attend His Freedom Reigns Ministries, where I give testimonies from time to time through life experiences and what the good Lord provides.

As I prepared this book for you, I stand before you broken, changed, and transformed. About six months before writing this publication, I had a very powerful woman of God prophesize over me, telling me that I would be facing a very difficult challenge, and that the Lord was working on me, breaking me down, changing me, and transforming me. She said that I shouldn't lose faith during this time period, that all would work out well in the end.

Well, in my profession, when a challenge comes along, you grab it by the horns. And, there was no difference in this. When I returned to work, I started jumping every call that sounded good. I wasn't going to miss this opportunity to prove my faith is strong in the Lord. After about a week and a half, I still had not been challenged, and I was starting to think that I must have missed it. Then one of my children grew ill, and was lonely and needing some fatherly time, so I went home early to spend time with this child.

While I was spending time with my child, my wife told me that she had to leave to go to work, and that I needed to move my car, since I was parked behind her. So I hurried out to move my car, and twisted my ankle. My ankle went one way, and I went the other, and down I went. After having some personal testimony in the yard, I dragged myself back into the house, and had my wife look at the problem. She decided that I needed to go to the hospital.

Well it turns out that there are three ligaments on the outside of the bone in your ankle. I shredded two of them. Who knows what happen to the other one. Have you ever heard the cliché', "The Lord works in mysterious ways?" Well, let me tell you, sometimes they hurt too.

So, here I was out of work. What was I going to do for the next few months? Well, I decided to start going to church more regular. Then on the very next Sunday, my pastor asked me to start giving messages on our Wednesday night services. So, that's what I did. I started reading and devouring the Bible.

Now, I once use to sin without care, who would drink alcoholic beverages after every shift, cuss up a storm because I thought it made me sound special, and gamble, playing poker on the Internet every night. In the process of shredding the ligaments in my foot, and the application of studying God's Word, I quit these vices. But, what's funny about this situation is that I didn't realize that I had quit. It took several weeks to realize that I had quit drinking and gambling, and I didn't miss it at all.

Now upon my return back to work, I realized that I had stop cursing, because as soon as I got mad about something, I cursed. Then the conviction of the Holy Spirit came upon me, and that's not a good feeling at all.

One would think that I had made great changes in my life over this six month time period. On April 4th, 2007, I told the Lord that I quit the use of tobacco, because I was tired of mistreating the Temple of the Holy Spirit. So I asked for help. Then after 28 years of using at least two cans of snuff a day, I walked away cold turkey.

During this same time period, my wife walked away from smoking for the last fifteen years, at three packs a day.

Something special, I think, must be going on here. Were we so strong that we were able to quit these vices without any problems? No! We didn't beat any of these problems by ourselves, the Lord beat them for us, and He gave us the power to take the stand, and quit for good.

So why did this happen to my family and me over this six month time period? Because now is the time. We, as a whole, are a stiff necked, high-minded society that always seems to need visual and physical proof to believe something. We are so caught up in the daily activities of the carnal world that we sometimes forget to fellowship with the Lord. We sometimes place Him on the back burner till later.

Have you seen the signs? They have started. Hurricane Katrina, 9/11, two different Tsunami's, and what about the Virginia Tech campus shooting just this week? These are just the beginning, and many, many more will come. What can we do about it? What are we to do?

Well, Jesus is calling. Can you hear him? Have you heard him? There is a revival going on right now in the church. That's what I got caught up in. Jesus is announcing himself to his people in this revival. He is calling his people to come forth and start bearing fruit.

Now what do I mean by that? Jesus is calling, and now is the time to answer. He is calling his people forward, to start bearing fruit. Everybody is called. Everybody is called to preach. Joyce Meyers and Benny Hinn have been called to preach on major television shows, and Pastor Barbara Cannon has been called to preach from the pulpit of His Freedom Reigns Ministries. I have been called to preach from the pulpit of my patrol car. We have all been called to preach from our position in life. We can't all have a television show. The preaching on the television is for catching those large portions of the Lord's people using the big nets. We on the smaller circuit have been called to catch the ones that fell out of those big nets. Our pulpit consists of where ever we are in our daily walk with God.

How do you know that you have been called? Because the Bible says it is so. In the Book of Mark 16:15-16, Jesus stated,

> *"Go into all the world and preach the gospel to every creature. He who believes and is baptized will be saved; but he who does not believe will be condemned."*

This is called the Great Commission. When Jesus stated it, it was basically an order, not a suggestion. Too many people in today's society interpret this scripture as a suggestion on Jesus' behalf.

We are called to tell the greatest story ever. The story of the life, death, and resurrection of our Lord

Jesus Christ. This is exactly what we are here to boldly proclaim. God has a specific plan, a purpose for each and every one of us. This is designed in his Infinite plan, his perfect plan. We are each given an assignment, yet he will not make us do it. We have to choose to do it. We are each here for a purpose. Our purpose might be to witness to another, and bring them to Jesus Christ. We might have a purpose to rear our children up for special assignment. We might be here to lead entire congregations. But we can't get anywhere in the Lord's great plan if we close ourselves off from his guidance, and his wisdom.

It all starts with how we handle ourselves, both in private and in the public eye. If we truly trusted in God, we wouldn't have to worry about what others thought about us. Our actions and how we handle ourselves would promote God here on Earth, and we could then allow God to take care of us, like he has already promised to do.

By you picking up this book, I assume that you already question your own inner peace, or question how strong your relationship is with God. While reading this book, it is my prayer that I will be able to assist you to recognize and accept that we all have our own problems that we have to deal with, while living in the flesh world. I believe that as we study together, we will find that these problems help create these sins of the mind and help create a hostile environment for our physical and spiritual survival. These actions cause our life in the flesh to be in disarray, and disorder, thus forbidding our graduation of becoming more spiritually complete. With an open mind and a diligence on your part, we will be able to identify these areas of concern.

After we recognize and identify these areas of concern, then and only then will we be able to spiritually grow from there.

During our spiritual growth, we will take steps through mental and physical accomplishments to develop a new rationale of thinking for your flesh man, and for your spiritual man, through learning to live with our conscience and develop peace of mind. This new rationale of thinking will assist us in living in this flesh world, while prospering in the spiritual realm.

Upon completion, I pray that we will be able to press forward in our relationship with the Lord, never looking back at the old self. When we start acting in our newfound self, we will be able to do away with the problems and concerns of our old self. During this new way of thinking, we will prosper in our relationships, both in a personal and professional manner. As we press forward, living through giving, we will grow closer to the Lord, and stronger in our faith, as we build our own unbreakable bond with God.

For the last nineteen years, I have been answering the call in today's society, in the capacity as a police officer. During my time in law enforcement, I have had to follow a strict set of standard operating procedures. Now its time to follow the guidelines that Jesus has in place. It's time to answer the Call of God.

It is my hope and desire that you enjoy reading this publication, and take something away from it in a positive manner, helping you become stronger in Christ than you were before. God bless you all, and please do what the Lord has asked you to do…. "Answer the Call."

Chapter One

Recognizing and Accepting the Problem

One of the hardest things to do in today's society, in my opinion, while living by the laws of spirit, and being surrounded by people living by the laws of the flesh, is to maintain control of your inner peace. Take for example my occupation, law enforcement. You would think that taking the streets and fighting evil and evil-doers, with helping people as much as possible would be stressful enough for anyone. But law enforcement is one of the deepest political games that there is. While helping protect and serving the community on the streets, you have to watch your back because you never know what is taking place behind your back within your own organization. So during these political games that surround you at work, how does one survive. First, as a Christian, you choose not to participate in these games. But, by not taking a side for or against, you have chose to become a target for both. What is the right approach? The right approach is to maintain focus on your Christian lifestyle, and to live your life in an effort to be able to hold your head upright in the path that the Lord has paved for you. At some point in time, your actions, or lack there of, will offend someone, and someone else's actions will offend you in your beliefs. You might allow this to breed fear in you, from taking actions or even causing you to look elsewhere for another occupation. But, of course, this example doesn't only apply to work, but to life in general. That brings me to an answer that I found in the Bible.

In the Book of 1 John 4:18, it states,

"There is no fear in love, but perfect love casts out fear, because fear involves torment. But he who fears has not been made perfect in love."

This verse has a deep meaning to how we all should live our lives. If this love of Christ is in us, we will find we have no fear. We will have no nervous condition, because it will vanish. When you have fear, it is imperfect love...it is a departure from the inner circle of the faith of God. Because of God's love, we transform into fearless confidence toward God and your brothers and sisters in Christ.

Instead of allowing actions of others to affect us, we must maintain our inner peace, that personal relationship that we hold with the Lord. Therefore, instead of standing by, allowing others to take action, we should take an active role, and demonstrate our lifestyle and become an active witness for the Lord. If we take the initial stance not to waver, and not to give up our personal relationship with the Lord, we affect others by our actions and our lifestyle. Once our active role is apparent to others, it causes them to make a difficult decision. They have to choose whether to fight against the power of the Lord in us all, or to leave us alone, and out of the games that they play, or lastly, and what we should want, to join us in our perfect love that we share with God.

By holding true to the Word of the Lord, we are able to maintain an inward bond of peace with another child of God. A bond that is made possible by the love of God, which is a perfect love. It is love that was demonstrated by our Lord Jesus Christ. If we can live this lifestyle in all that we do, we can act as a catalyst, that will ignite the flow of our father's love, and help transform people on a daily basis.

Now, during these times where I find myself driving from call to call, and doing all the aspects of my job, my mind has the availability to create all kinds of suspicions, which allows my mind to create doubt about my own self, and my own future.

All thoughts that come from the mind are generally directed toward things over the Earth in the flesh world, and by living in the flesh world it is impossible to raise these thoughts all the way up to heaven. When we are thinking, there is a corresponding action driven from the heart. This is where we create such emotions like; anger, envy, fear, joy, hope, and despair. When we lack inner peace, this allows us to create disorder in our lives, not only in our thoughts, but also in our emotions. With our thoughts jump-starting our emotions, it connects our mind to our heart. This allows our emotions to take control of our lives, thus overpowering our own conscience. When this occurs, we can't expect to have any kind of peaceful life because we have lost touch with our inner peace.

For instance, while driving down the road and someone cuts you off in traffic almost causing an accident, are you angry, allowing your flesh to take control as you give them your absolute best hand gesture, and/or screaming at them at the top of your lungs? Now they can't hear you, and hopefully they can't see you, because both of those reactions can only lead to further problems. Problems like embarrassment in front of your family, an actual fistfight, and police involvement. And the appropriate reaction should be thankfulness for your God given ability to avoid this collision. Can you see in this one example how your emotions dictate your physical (flesh) reaction? The first two reactions give into your flesh and thus allowing you to lose your inner peace and your connection with God. The last reaction allows your to spiritually thank God for your life and your skills, and demonstrates your patience and mercy that you have extended to your fellow man, whom may or may not have seen you. If we give into the flesh, and allow our flesh to react, we will become shocked and amazed that our own reaction will generally lead us into a far worse situation. The worst situation that I am talking about is police involvement, physical altercation, embarrassment in front of our family, and even death.

The thoughts that we cherish, emotions, and desires that are all within us, drive us to give in to improper actions. These actions, on our part, are caused by our conscience losing power, and control of its place in our life, and are sidelined. Picture this in the image of a football team. Our conscience is the starting Quarterback, a veteran on our team. When we let our emotions run rampant in our lives, it is like benching the star quarterback, and letting the water boy play instead. Our conscience has been with us from the start. The more powerful our conscience is, the more likely it will steer us toward making the right decisions, in our thoughts and reactions.

To bring this into perspective,

we find in the Book of Isaiah 55:7-8, it states,

"Let the wicked forsake his way, and the unrighteous man his thoughts; Let him return to the Lord, And He will have mercy on him; And to our God,

For He will abundantly pardon. For my thoughts are not your thoughts, Nor are your ways My ways, says the Lord."

In reading these verses, it states that the wicked will forsake themselves and lose out on the greatest gift known to man. However, it goes on to say that even when we make a mistake, we can still repent, and be forgiven. As you struggle to get your flesh under control, you will make mistakes. Isn't it wonderful that God will still forgive you of these mistakes, to where you can still receive the joy, peace, and everlasting life promised to you by the Father?

One of the greatest principles of the Christian life is forgiveness. Jesus lived this principle daily. While hanging on the cross, he prayed for the people who put him there. His words were so powerful that they brought the conversion of one of the thieves that was hanging on the cross with him. God promises us his forgiveness. (Supported by 1 John 1:9) Now if the Lord can forgive our transgressions, who are we that can't do the same. Are we really so prim and proper in ourselves that we never offend anyone, and are allowed to hold grudges.

As a police officer for the last nineteen years, I have seen a lot of things that I would rather forget. However, when talking about inner peace, it has been my experience that police officers go from call to call listening to other people's problems and trying to solve them; yet it doesn't stop there. Police Officers, as an example, take other people's problem to heart. They don't do this intentionally, but police officers are human too. They generally end up taking a problem or two with them. This creates problems in their own inner peace, and it wasn't their problem to start with. And this problem doesn't just occur in the lives of police officers. It occurs everywhere.

People, who supervise others, fall into the category as well. A supervisor, when counseling an employee, places himself in jeopardy of accepting the problems of the other that can ruin their own inner peace. Then, the supervisor can also take it a step further, and can allow that problem to create the wrong image of that employee, thus ruining the relationship between them. This kind of reaction can end up jeopardizing a career, by labeling that employee as trouble.

In my time as a police officer, I have had to deal with a wide assortment of calls such as driving under the influence accidents, fatality accidents, domestic violence cases, and murder. In these examples, it would be easy to take some of these issues home with you that could cloud your own issues and create more problems than they should.

Now what do these examples mean to you. Well, a disturbed spirit can't follow and be totally dependant on the Lord because the problems of the flesh keep one away from the promise and peace of God. In these examples, I have shown that it is very easy, while dealing in the flesh, to accept someone else's burden. When you accept someone else's burden, you cheat yourself out of the truly blessed relationship that you can have with the Lord. In the flesh, these additional burdens that you accept damper you lifestyle that you lead because you hinder your personal relationships with family and friends. But, I will show you how to deal with this problem. First, we refer to God because God has given us the way to relieve this burden.

In the Book of 1 Peter 5:6-7, it states,

"Therefore humble yourselves under the mighty hand of God, that He may exalt you in due time,

casting all your care upon Him, for He cares for you."

So what does this scripture say to us? When you break it down, it shows that we, as children of God, need to take our worries, burdens, anxieties, and distractions, to the Father. This kind of worry is unnecessary in our daily life because the Father's love provides for both our daily and our personal needs.

What happens if we take on these other burdens, and keeps them as our own, without any type of resolution or resolve? Well, when these additional burdens, or the normal burden's that we have in our daily life are too much for us; they change us. They begin to dictate how we live. These burdens have changed our inner peace, to where we are in a state of confusion, and out of the will of God. Because you have lost your inner peace, you are now not moving forward in your walk with God. You may not have sinned, but you lack the opportunity to progress forward, and increase in your relationship with God. And we know that if you are not progressing forward with God, then you are a backslider.

What does it mean to be a backslider? Backsliding is turning back, turning away; defecting, faithlessness, disloyalty, reverting. If repentance is a turning around, backsliding is a turning back, or turning away from God. Backsliding is addressed in the Bible as well,

and in the Book of Jeremiah 3:22, it states,

"Return, you backsliding children, And I will heal your backsliding. Indeed we do come to You, For You are the Lord our God."

As specified in Jeremiah 3:22, it states that God regards backsliding as a condition, that requires God's healing. If our relationship is such that requires healing at this point, then are we covered by the Lord's love, or have we lost ourselves? I believe that when we reach a situation, a backsliding, that we should immediately turn to the Lord for this divine healing. We need to walk closer with the Lord everyday. A moment without His grace, gives the devil too much opportunity to destroy what is precious in your life. When you are dealing with more than you can handle, turn it over to the Lord.

In Book of Psalms 55:22, it states,

"Cast your burden on the Lord, And He shall sustain you; He shall never permit the righteous to be moved."

Now that is pretty nice. It states in that scripture, to cast your burdens on the Lord, and He will keep you up. God is able to take them, and He desires to carry your burdens for you. You do not have the skills necessary to fight every fight by yourself. Turn your problems over to the Lord. He is strong enough to handle your issues, your mistakes, and to bring you back into his protection. If you chose to handle these problems by yourself, you are basically turning your back on God. Take your problems to the Father, he will carry them, and provide for you as well.

I think that it is safe to say that we, meaning human beings, are all trying to satisfy our flesh self, our outer needs, but that is not really what we need to be happy. I think we first need to locate and develop something that we lost, while we were growing up in this flesh world. We all should be trying to find our inner peace. For the most part, we are born and reared to live in inner peace. The external pressures of society changed that, and we end up losing ourselves, because we start to conform to what other people want us to be. When we recognize that we have been placed off balance, we desperately start searching for our lost world, but we keep looking in the wrong place. Inner peace, that is real peace, can not be found in society today through other people and material items, but has to be found within us, potentially lost under years and years of garbage piled on from the external factors that we have to deal with in our daily lives.

To find this inner peace that was lost, we need to seek God's assistance. We have to be broken down, changed, and transformed by God, inside ourselves, so that God can work in us from within to make us spiritually stronger, which in turn will allow us to gain control of our flesh. Imagine picking out a horse from the wilderness. When you chose one, would you jump on the horses back immediately, and start riding, or would you want that horse to be broken, and changed to conform to the needs that you have. This is the same thing that needs to happen to us. We need to allow God to break us down, change us, and transform us into someone who has control over their flesh, and can chose to live spiritually, rather than by the laws of the flesh. A prime example of this transformation in related from the Bible in the Book of Genesis, where it tells of Jacob and his brother Esau.

In Genesis 32:24-26 it states,

"Then Jacob was left alone; a man wrestled with him until the breaking of day. Now when He saw that He did not prevail against him, He touched the socket of his hip; and the socket of Jacob's hip was out of joint as he wrestled with Him. And He said,

"Let me go, for the day breaks, but he said I will not let you go unless you bless me."

The importance of this narrative is that Jacob's display showed a willingness to do what it took to get God's attention, in his most desperate time of need. He would not settle for anything less than a blessing from the Lord. This wrestling is not physical, but spiritual in nature for through his repentance, Jacob's prayers were answered. God showed Jacob his face, the ultimate answer that changed Jacob's life forever.

Most of our inner peace problems can be filed into one of the seven deadly sins. If you don't remember what the seven deadly sins are they are as follows: Gluttony, Lust, Greed, Sloth, Wrath, Envy, and Pride. Each issue that continues to keep us away from God's given right to inner peace has been around since the beginning of the Bible. These seven deadly sins are man-made and are not divine in nature. These sins start to work on us through our mind, and that is where the devil starts attacking. These seven deadly sins, which I will call obstacles, start in the mind.

Now you might say that some of these obstacles start in the heart, but I disagree. These obstacles start in the mind, and we allow them to transfer to the heart. We use that feeling we get from the heart, to give us the courage to act on our thoughts. But the answer is simple. When we accept God into our lives, he lives in our heart. Since this is so precious, we will learn to turn our mind off from these obstacles, and we can disregard these ideas. That is why the devil doesn't attack our heart. He can't. He has no power over God. He won't be able to get into our heart, unless we allow him that privilege. Think of it this way. Our mind is like the doorway to a house. This doorway that I am talking about is the doorway of our body, our life. The devil enters through the doorway of our mind, in an effort to take over and enter into our heart. Our heart is where the Lord lives. My heart doesn't have enough room for both. Do not let the devil in; the Lord doesn't need to be replaced. And the last time I checked, the Lord doesn't want a roommate.

Can you hold on like Jacob did? You certainly can if you are sincere, and are dependant, broken and weak. It is when you are weak that Jesus is strong in you. (2Corintians 12:9) This is one of God's greatest promises. On the other hand, if you are self-minded, self-righteous, if you are proud, or high-minded, or are puffed up in your own mind, you can receive nothing from him. I am absolutely nothing without the power and the anointing of the Holy Spirit. It is through a life of dependence that there is a life of power. If you are not there, get alone with God. If you must, spend the whole day and/or night with God, and let him change and transform you. Never let him go until he blesses you, until he makes you a prince of God.

Remember, Jesus completely forgave us; therefore, he wants us to follow his example by forgiving others. Remember that forgiveness first comes from God. The Lord's forgiveness knows no limits, therefore, ours shouldn't either, for if it does, aren't we elevating ourselves above our Lord, which is ridiculous. The Lord's forgiveness is not selective, and the Lord's forgiveness breaks down walls. Once you experience this kind of forgiveness, you can become truly free in Christ. With this kind of peace of mind, what could be better? Can you do better on your own?

In the Book of Ephesians 4:31 thru 5:2, the Bible reflects the correct mindset. I suggest you study this later, but for now, I will give you the bare bones of this message. We are to get rid of all bitterness, rage, anger, harsh words, and slander, as well as all types of malicious behavior. Instead, be kind to each other, tenderhearted, forgiving one another, just as God, through Christ has forgiven you and I. Following God's example in everything we do, because we are his dear children. We should live a life filled with love for others, following the example of Christ, who loved you and I and gave himself as a sacrifice to take away our sins. And this action allows us to find the joy, peace and eternal life that God intended us to have. If we can complete this, we will find a love like no other, and a fellowship with the Father, that can't be compared to anything known to man.

If these examples and my thoughts have stirred you, to where you can identify that you have issues that need direct attention. Let's move forward in this book. Let's identify the areas of concern, and let's start changing them for the better. As we strive together, we will find that the good Lord can break us down, change and transform us not only into a better person here on Earth, but into a person who is on fire for God, then into a mighty powerful child of God. Together, we can take this journey. All it takes is a clear and open mind to what comes next, a willingness to accept some fault, a willingness to give yourself completely to the Lord, and a desire to walk with the Lord in love and fellowship.

Do you like what you hear? Do you want to be a better person? Do you want this kind of relationship with the Lord? Well, let's stop stalling and move on to the next chapter.

Chapter Two

Identifying the Areas of Concern

Congratulations! You have accomplished the hardest part of the recovery process. You should be proud of yourself. Recognizing and accepting that you have an inner peace problem is a hard step to take. Most people in this world refuse to accept such a thing. Even if they see, from time to time, that they have a problem, they choose to avoid the situation, or think that they can overcome their problem on their own, without any type of education, or assistance.

Now let's try to identify the areas that seem to affect us all. Most of these problem areas are identifiable through the attacks on our mind. When the devil attacks us, it is through our mind. The mind is an area that the devil plants different thoughts in to cause us, in the flesh world, to react.

When we come under attack, it is usually through the seven deadly sins. These seven deadly sins are man-made, and are utilized in the flesh world to prey on our natural fleshy instincts. The fleshy instincts are what cause us to become trapped in the sins of the world. The seven deadly sins are sins that separate us from God. Sins in themselves deeply root within us and can take over our lives, before we really understand what has happened.

To refresh our memory in this category, the seven deadly sins are Gluttony, Lust, Greed, Sloth, Wrath, Envy, and Pride. As you can see, these sins have been around the world ever since the devil has made this his playground. These sins attack the very nature of how this flesh world operates. As you can tell, most all of these sins are utilized to attack our mind, planting in us the need for improving ourselves, and our position in the world. This occurs in every occupation known to man.

In law enforcement, as previously stated, all these sins come in to play. Most all police officers want to improve in their individual chains of command, making higher rank, getting higher pay, and becoming more important in their individual assignments, or at least the thought in their minds.

To place proper perspective on each of these deadly sins, let's identify each by definition, and place some in a designated example in the flesh world. By doing this, we will be able to identify how easily these thoughts can creep into our individual minds, and take over our lives.

Gluttony

First, let's take Gluttony. Gluttony is the over indulgence and over consumption of food, drink, or intoxicants to the point of waste. It is a misplaced desire of food or even withholding from the needy. Gluttony makes one selfish. Gluttonous people will not share, since they seem to never get enough to satisfy their cravings. It seems like the things we crave in the flesh world, have no lasting value. Gluttonous activity leads to poverty. This act results in poverty in the flesh world, as well as the spiritual realm. A prime example of this kind of poverty is listed in the Bible. In the Book of Proverbs 23: 20-21, it states,

"Do not mix with winebibbers, or with gluttonous eaters of meat; For the drunkard and the glutton will come to poverty, And drowsiness will clothe a man with rags."

When interpreting these verses, we see that this is a warning from a father to a son. He is being told to watch and beware of envious sinners and hanging out with drunks, gluttons, and harlots. Now after being warned what not to do, what should we pay attention to? Well, we should fear the Lord, give attention to our parents, value the truth in all instances, and create a positive environment for our family.

We see this in all forms of addictions, and even the rich can lose it all. These kinds of activities can stop us from dealing with our problems, therefore; they increase. In law enforcement, alcoholism is probably one of the worst forms of Gluttony. The abuse of hard liquor and beer is my pet peeve in this area. I remember, before my wife brought me before my savior, that I would drink around a half a bottle of Gentleman Jack Daniels every morning when I got off of work. I used this to bring down my stamina and the adrenaline that would naturally occur at work. Of course, that was my story. I really was unhappy, and upset about some things that had occurred in my life, and didn't know how to deal with them. Fortunately, for me, I had friends that helped more than they will ever know, and my wife's participation is a blessing.

However, when we seek to have our cravings filled, we normally seek and take all that we desire from the flesh world. We start taking and taking, and taking, until one day we realize that we are still empty. We can never seem to get satisfied.

When we look for fulfillment, we again look into God's Word. In the Bible, from the Book of Isaiah 55:1-2, it states,

"Ho! Everyone who thirsts, Come to the waters; And you who have no money, Come, buy, and eat. Yes, come, buy wine and milk Without money and without price. Why do you spend money for what is not bread, And your wages for what does not satisfy? Listen carefully to me, and eat what is good, And let your soul delight itself in abundance."

These simple verses state that God's abundant life is free. God's abundant life is fulfilling. In this scripture, God is saying to come to the table. Eat the bread of life. Crave for the Lord; seek him with all your might. When we choose to seek real fulfillment, when we chose to fill our emptiness, we need to seek Jesus Christ. By seeking Jesus Christ, we find the answer to our emptiness, and then and only then, will we be truly satisfied.

Lust

Secondly, Lust is any intense desire or craving, usually sexual, although it is common to speak of as a lust for life, lust for blood, or a lust for power. It becomes a sin when it is an excess or inappropriately directed sexual desire, and is primarily a sin of excess. The Greek word Lust translates into English as "To Covet." It is an impulsive, passionate desire.

Lust is a form of passion, tainted by sin. Love is a marathon runner, and lust is running in the ten-yard dash. Lust never satisfies our need, and leads to greater perversion. When we refer to the Bible, we find in one of the many references of this subject in 1 Corinthians 6:18-20, where it states,

> *"Flee sexual immorality. Every sin that a man does is outside the body, but he who commits sexual immorality sins against his own body.*
> *Or do you not know that your body is the temple of the Holy Spirit*
> *Who is in you, whom you have from God, and you are not your own?*
> *For you were bought at a price; therefore glorify God in your body and*
> *In your spirit, which are God's.*

As we interpret these verses, we see that sexual immorality has far reaching effects that involve both great spiritual significance and social complications. We further find that immorality is a sin not only against our body, but also against the body of the Holy Spirit, who dwells within us all. Wow, that's pretty powerful. Your body is the temple of the Holy Spirit. This is brought to us by the price paid from Jesus Christ. Such a precious and tremendous gift, why would you ever want to damage something that is priceless?

Lust is described as an emotional taste of life, but since it is short lived, the thrill is gone immediately, and then we have to seek more. Lust can be found so prominently on television and in movies. It has become part of this society's culture, cultivated by our entertainment needs and desires of the flesh world. In the sexual arena, lust is a longing for sexual satisfaction outside of marriage. It has been described as an agitated longing, a frightening craving, and an out of touch desire for something, or someone that is not yours. Another scripture that we find in the Bible, in the Book of Matthew 5:27-28, and this time it is "Jesus" who states,

"You have heard that it was said to those of old, You shall not commit adultery! But I say to you that whoever looks at a woman to lust for her has already committed adultery with her in his heart."

This describes lust as a desire to possess, to own, to consume without caring about the needs, or feelings of any other being, or the will of God. So to break it down further, lust allows us to commit a deadly sin against the Temple of the Holy Spirit that is within us. This then changes our mind into absolutely not caring what anybody thinks about us. Which results where we don't care about the partner of the flesh that we have dragged down with us.

If you need a better example of lust, and how it can affect your personal and professional life, look in the newspaper, or check the Internet for news stories under the category of sexual harassment. It is everywhere. It is destroying both the primary aggressor's and the victim's alike. It creates a hostile work environment, where the end result is your being fired, your being sued, or your victim's life changing so much that they might lose touch with everything that was important to them. Of course, these are mostly financial considerations. What about the mentality that gets changed? These changes occur, and end up hurting or destroying one of our brothers or sisters in Christ.

Lust is a hidden sin. If this sin isn't hidden, then that person is lost in the perversion of his or her own mind. So lost, that it would take divine healing to bring them back to the Lord. It operates behind the scenes and in secret. This adds to the hidden illusion of satisfaction. Who can tell what is on our minds? Besides us, only the Lord our God can read our mind and thoughts. He can see right down into our hearts and minds and sees how we think and what we are going to do.

Greed

Thirdly, Greed is called a selfish desire to obtain money, wealth, material possessions, or any other entity more than one legitimately needs. Greed is pretty easy to understand in today's society. Television and movies have exploited greed for entertainment purposes. However even with their representing greed sometimes in a negative context, we in our society still have it as a problem.

Take for example the story of Cain and his brother Abel. I won't go into great detail quoting the Bible, but I refer you to the Book of Genesis 4:8 for the complete story. In this story, Cain becomes jealous of his brother Abel and his relationship with God. Due to his greed for more from the Lord, he gave into human temptations and committed murder. As you can see in this story, greed creates the wrong way of life. Like Cain, instead of following God, he chose a self-serving purpose for himself. Faith in your own self is not the way. The way of Greed leads only to sin, death, emptiness, and heartache. As with Cain, it leads to murder, a loss of family, and desolation.

Greed undermines God's authority. Greed then produces the wrong motivation for life. As it is quoted in scriptures, we find in the Book of Proverbs 15:27, it states,

"He who is greedy for gain troubles his own house,
But he who hates bribes will live."

We see in interpreting this scripture that if we give into troubling ourselves for gain through greedy means and motives, this brings only more grief to ourselves, and our homes, which includes our families. Greed pushes us to live our life for personal gain through the misuse of God's provisions. Therefore, Greed establishes the wrong authority in life.

When looking for another story from the Bible to study out for the area of Greed, we see in the Book of Luke 12:13-21, we see that Jesus had occasion to be asked to settle a civil dispute, however, he chose not to settle the dispute, but turned the situation around into a learning exercise for the people involved. I would suggest that you study this out yourself, and you will find that the moral to this lesson that Jesus was teaching us is that true life has nothing to do with possessions. The sin of Greed is directed toward the acquisition of more possessions and, this, is self-defeating and futile. It does not know the meaning of life. To support this lesson, we find in the Book of Proverbs 1:19, where it states,

"So are the ways of everyone who is greedy for gain;
It takes away the life of its owners."

By this scripture, we find support for Jesus' lesson that came later in the Book of Luke, where we find that possessions neither give life, nor provide security, because death separates us from material things. So how do we escape the stranglehold of Greed? *Be loyal to God. Forsake any ambitions that compromise your commitment to God.*

Sloth

The fourth sin is Sloth. Sloth translates into laziness. Sloth is a lack of desire to act or work in general to do an act or work that is expected of a person. Procrastination qualifies under the heading of Sloth.

Sloth is a sin that believes in nothing. The church can become slothful in their action, or lack thereof. Churches can become complacent or lukewarm in their efforts to fulfill God's Will. The question of laziness is primarily used in today's society for the church. This category is utilized to motivate congregations to become active Christians, instead of straddling the fence. When looking for support in the Bible for the individual, we see in the Book of Proverbs 24:30-34, it states,

> *"I went by the field of the lazy man, And by the vineyard of the man devoid of understanding; And there it was, all overgrown with thorns;*
>
> *Its surface was covered with nettles; Its stone wall was broken down.*
>
> *When I saw it, I considered it well; I looked on it and received instruction; A little sleep, a little slumber, a little folding of the hands to rest; So shall your poverty come like a prowler, And your need like an armed man."*

As we see the author is relating that the man in this portion of the story makes clear the tragedy of idleness. Slothfulness, or laziness is condemned in passivity, or a lack of initiative, or the habit of procrastination. When we participate in this kind of activity, we become oblivious to the dire results that follow, because of our lack of discipline.

When we allow sloth, or laziness, if you prefer, to enter into our personal lives, we become lazy and non-caring about things that make us who we are. With the addition of laziness in our personal lives, we cease to make progress in all things that are, or were, important to us. This transfers over to our professional life, damaging all the hope and promise that has been created. When laziness takes over, our relationship with the Lord is damaged. We cease to press forward, seeking him, and never maturing into the powerful men and women of God, the Lord wants in all of us.

Sloth, or laziness, placed in a real live example. I will describe how laziness can creep into the life of a police officer. Law enforcement is a job that requires total concentration from the time you put on the uniform till the time you take it off. It doesn't start when you clock in or out. You become a target once you leave your home, until you return after work, because of the uniform, or the take home car privilege. After nineteen years, I find, from time to time, that I can become complacent in my occupation. My mind sometimes wanders into thoughts like, I've did this so long, I'm just going to ride around and hang out today. If they need me, they'll call, however, I'm not going to get out here and bust my butt. I'm a veteran; I have earned the right to slack off.

Now you can see that this is not just associated in law enforcement. It can happen in any occupation out there. But in my example, I have slacked off, and not provided my all. I have let down my supervisors, my peers, and my subordinates. I have also let down the public that I serve. Can you think of anybody else that I have let down? I have let down my family, and even let down myself. After a while, the complacency instills in your demeanor, and you become lost in a void of delusional service.

Wrath

The fifth is Wrath. Wrath, which is also anger, is an emotional response to a grievance. The grievance may appear to be real, or imagined, it may have its roots in a past, present experience, or it may be anticipated of a future event. Anger is invariably based on the perception of threat, or a perceived threat due to a conflict, injuring, negligence, humiliation, and betrayal among others.

Wrath is described more commonly in today's society as anger. Anger commonly used in the form of verbal and physical assaults, as well as, silent anger that ends up growing in to a potential unstoppable force within you. We can even list in the category of Wrath with having, displaying, and living with a bad attitude. We find in the Bible listed in the Book of 1 John 3:13-15, where it states,

> *"Do not marvel, my brethren, if the world hates you. We know that we have passed from death to life, because we love the brethren. He who does not love his brother abides in death. Whoever hates his brother is a murderer, and you know that no murderer has eternal life abiding in him."*

In interpreting these verses, we see that love is the characteristics of a Christian believer for all his fellow brother and sisters in the Lord, and is displayed in our daily righteous living. As the scripture states, don't be happy if your persona has made it to where the world hates you, for you have therefore, alienated yourself from love, which is the key to eternal life.

Anger is a form of murder, because of its desire to destroy anyone who blocks the path in obtaining the satis-faction wanted, or who assaults us, or makes us look bad, whether in public or in our private life. When we check God's word again we see that in the Book of Ephesians 4:26-27, it states,

> *"Be angry, and do not sin: do not let the sun go down on your wrath, nor give place to the devil."*

In interpreting these verses, it shows the outcome of our anger can sometimes win the moment that we are in, however, it is not allowed to win the whole day. If we maintain our anger the whole of day, we give ground to Satan, and he gains control over a portion of our life.

Unresolved anger can produce depression, physical and verbal outburst, and can cause to fear, and/or become alienated from others, often times away from our friends and loved ones. When we have this alienation, our friends and families take the brunt of our hostilities, even though it was not directed toward them to start with.

Envy

The sixth is Envy. Envy is an emotion that occurs when a person lacks another's superior quality, achievement, or possession and desires it or wishes that the other lacked it. It is considered sinful because envious people ignore their own blessings, and focus on others status rather than their own spiritual growth.

Envy is a painful or resentful awareness of an advantage enjoyed by another, joined with the desire to possess the same. Envy brings disorder. It divides and sets us apart and against each other.

Envy kills contentment, as it slowly siphons the joy out of our life. It leads us astray from enjoying what we have. It rots our reasoning and ruins our relationship with others. As we look in the Bible, we find in the Book of James 3:16-18, it states,

"For where envy and self-seeking exist, confusion and every evil thing are there. But wisdom that is from above is first pure, then peaceable, gentle, willing to yield, full of mercy and good fruits, without partiality and without hypocrisy. Now the fruit of righteousness is sown in peace by those who make peace."

While interpreting these verses we see that we must fully love God. He is always reliable, if we are worthy. Confusion and dissension result as God begins to remove his blessings from our efforts, removing his flow of grace. Remember that every gift the Lord gives to us is good and perfect for us in his divine plan.

Envy ruins our ability to reason out thoughts in our mind, which in turn teaches us to resent God's decision to bless someone or something we want or think we deserve.

Envy is one of the most prevalent characteristics in today's society. It is even used in commercial advertisements to get us to sway toward things, materialistic things that we may not really need. While doing this it cripples our relationship with God. We lose trust in him along with our spiritual growth.

In the Book of Proverbs 14:30, it states,

"A sound heart is life to the body, But envy is rottenness to the bones."

A mind at peace brings forth good physical health. When we are envious of others, it ruins our physical and spiritual healthiness. Envy left unchecked, becomes a catalyst of every other evil thought and action. It can cause us to become ill, and unhappy, while crippling our ability to enjoy what we have, and destroying our ability to be thankful for what we have.

To place envy into perspective in the real world, imagine that you and your friend started working at your company at the same time. Yet, your friend received a promotion, he or she received a better workstation or office, or some other perks that can add up. Before we start trying to find out what he or she accomplished, in an effort to better ourselves, we start to question, why they received the special treatment, and we didn't. Why are they getting special incentives, when we are doing the same kind of work? This type of thinking, with the addition of pride can lead us into a hostile work environment. A work environment that we create, that which could eventually lead to our being fired from the job, losing quality friends, and earning a bad reputation, which could lead to making it impossible to find another job to help provide for our families.

This type of thinking occurs all the time in law enforcement. The questions of why did he receive the promotion and I didn't? Why did they pick that person for the special assignment, and not me? What do they have that I don't? They picked the other people because I don't play ball, I don't suck up, or the other people is in their special group. This kind of thinking will end up destroying your working relationship with everybody, and could ultimately end up destroying your reputation, and relationship with others, including your family and friends.

Pride

The last is Pride. Pride refers to a strong sense of self-respect, a refusal to be humiliated as well as joy in the accomplishment of oneself. It also means excessive pride, which was usually the defining trait that leads to the tragic hero's downfall according to Aristotle. Excessive pride also manifests itself as arrogance, the act of obtaining rights or advantages including vainglorious or rhetorical advantage sometimes through violence or that of violence. Pride is essentially competitive and excessive belief in one's own ability that interferes with the individual's recognition of the grace of God, or the worth, which God sees in others.

We live in a world where everyone brags about their own self, and building themselves up and declaring their own accomplishments just to get noticed. You might ask why anyone would act in such a manner. If you have ever received a bit of praise, then you know how intoxicating that pride can be. It reminds me of the parable of Taking the Lowly Place, written in the Book of Luke 14:7-11, where Jesus rebukes social pride. It is written in verse 11, where it states, and Jesus said,

"For whoever exalts himself will be humbled, and he who humbles himself will be exalted."

This lesson teaches us that our unselfish motives in performing deeds of kindness will not go unnoticed. Even if our acts go unnoticed at the moment, they are written down in the Lamb's Book of Life, and will accompany you on Judgment Day. Also in this parable he shows that God honors those who recognize their own lowliness and unworthiness. In recognizing their weaknesses they turn to God and rely solely on God's Mercy.

Pride becomes sinful when it begins to cause a feeling of superiority over other people. When it inflates who we are, and what we have done. It becomes part of your consciousness, where you walk, talk, and act as if you are puffed up in your own mind. If you need further example, we see in the Book of Proverbs 8:13, where it states,

"The fear of the Lord is to hate evil; Pride and arrogance and the evil way And the perverse mouth I hate."

The Lord hates EVIL. There are four things listed that the Lord hates. They are Evil, The Evil Way, Arrogance, and Pride. Pride acts as the gateway to just about every other sin, and it sets up a barrier between us, and God, between our will and God's Will. Of course, it doesn't take an expert to figure out that pride ruins our conception of what is best for us. If we think our will is better for us than God's Will, we are desperately in need of divine help.

Pride is a problem. Some pride is actually good in the sense it drives us to become better, or to strive harder to accomplish our goals. However, I am going to describe in an example how pride got the best of me once. As a supervisor, I had received the Officer of the Month award a few times, and received the yearly Leadership award three or four times. Each time that I missed receiving one of these, because it is very hard to earn them year after year, I would find myself questioning why I didn't get the recognition that I deserved. Each time I won an award, I would find myself walking around all pumped up in my mind. Thinking that I was "It". I was the best cop around. But, with hindsight being 20/20, I realized later that I had only received these awards for doing the job that I agreed to do. Timing, and good fortune played a very important role in my receiving these awards. And I missed the opportunity to just be thankful to be alive, and my accomplishments that made a positive difference at one time or another.

Unfortunately, our prideful attitude will always be obvious by our actions. So when deciding on how to deal with the sin of pride, just remember, pride is the sin that got Satan kicked out of heaven.

Now that we have identified by definition the seven deadly sins, we should be able to realize how they affect our daily lives. These sins don't chose to rattle us only in our personal life, but affect our professional life as well. Take your time in this chapter. If you are unclear on any of the definitions, please review the information provided, and check other sources as well. As you ponder each sin, check your memory and see if they have already been prevalent in your life. Once you have a firm grasp on this area, move on and let's start taking the steps necessary to fix our problems, and start pressing closer to the Lord.

Chapter Three

Cleaning Out the Closet

To understand the new concept of walking with God, we have some rebuilding to do. The rebuilding process sounds like it is some sort of major undertaking, however, as time goes on, it will become easier and easier for you. But, like most changes that take place, the first steps will be hard. Just remember, like an infant taking their first steps, expect to fall down a couple of times. There will be a little pain involved to start with, both from personal sacrifices that you have to make, and from the associations that you had before you accepted Christ as your savior.

In my experience, I have found that the personal sacrifices are nothing in comparison to what Christ did for you and I on the cross, and the associations that I had before do not compare to the love I receive from Christ. My past associations are nothing to me if those people can't accept the changes that I have made in my personal self, my lifestyle, and how I handle myself in all aspects of life. These friends and acquaintances are not really worth having, if they are not accepting of me, how I am and chose to be.

Cleansing

When we start cleansing ourselves, and getting rid of all the fleshy things that we have accepted and adapted to our life, we should start with our own minds. Our minds influence who we are, how we act, or react, after many, many years of programming. It started when we were children and continues all the way up through adulthood. Our parents, the schools, and our own government, all have shared in programming us into what we are today. Normally our conscious allows us to feel good or bad depending on the decisions that we have made. The problem is that we don't always make good decisions. Our subconscious is usually our moral evaluator. It usually judges what we think and how we act based on our upbringing. The "How We Think" and the "How We React" tells a great deal of how we handle ourselves and how we handle interaction with people before we started and after we have taken the steps in our Christian walk with God.

In looking for guidance, or help if you will, in changing our thought process, we should first look to God's Word to start with. If you will refer to The Book of Ephesians 4 verses 17-24, you will find that God's Word shows that we should rid our minds of worthless thoughts and stubbornness, because that leads to a hardened heart. And remember that one with a hardened heart can't love, and without love, how can you experience the love of God.

We should rid our minds of all vices and deceitful desires as well as all indecent things. When you look within yourself, you have to evaluate these thoughts and ideas within, and decide what is appropriate, and what is not.

We have to adjust our mind set from automatically reacting with bitterness, rage, and anger. Then we have to stop telling lies. Telling lies has become such a common thing in today's society, that stopping will be very hard. Lying has become socially acceptable for the most part in relationships, in work, and has become part of our culture. Imagine if we could all change the lying pattern that has become so apparent in society today? Would we be better off? I think so.

And we should change ourselves from using insults and feelings of hate, which are commonly used to protect ourselves from others when we have feelings of anger, resentment, and fear. These responses are defense mechanisms, utilized to protect us from being hurt, and can be associated in other terms as damage control.

But, what we will find is that once we start these changes, people will start to see us in a new way. They will respond to our changes, positively, or they will break connection from us because we have made them uncomfortable in their own selves. Now this sounds potentially bad however, if our friends and associates will not accept us for who we are, were they really our friends to start with? If you choose to change, and your spouse doesn't chose to change or accept your new self, are they really a partner, or was this some type of control?

To explain some of these ideas listed above through examples from my own life, I was known for being kind of a dirty mouthed, insulting joker, who would down grade someone in front of their peers; basically insulting and embarrassing anyone to prove my point at the time. When people hung around me, they could expect to hear me cussing, talking about drinking, and talk about gambling in just about every conversation. See, before I started my walk with God, I liked to cuss. I thought at the time that made me sound big and bad...important if you will. I liked to drink. Gentleman Jack and cola was my drink. And for some reason, I wanted everyone to know this and know when I would be partaking. Then, the gambling, I liked to play poker on the Internet, and even in real life. When the poker games on the internet were not enough, or I couldn't get enough people to come over and play; I would schedule a trip to the closest casino.

But, when I started my walk with God, I changed. Now, I am not going to say that I was strong enough to make all the changes myself. I am sure that the good Lord stepped in and helped me tremendously in all these areas. And, when I started reading the Bible daily, I lost the urge to play poker. I lost the urge to drink alcoholic beverages, and I have stopped a majority of the cussing. I am no saint, because I slip every now and then, just like you will. But, I have made great improvements over time with the Lord's help, and strive to improve daily.

After my injury, I returned to work. When I returned to work, I had a couple of occasions where I could witness to others. I had opportunities to share my story with others, and potentially change them, or show them the way. But, I noticed that the more I showed my new self to others, the more I would hear comments that were made remarking about the tremendous change that was so apparent in my life. These changes that were made were all favorable. Most everyone liked the changes. As a matter of fact, I believe, I have more friends now than before my becoming saved. The friends or associates that I have lost, I realized, were truly not my friends at all, but associates that I still have, but in a weaker context, because of the vices and hindrances that I accepted in my life before Jesus.

The point of my personal example is not to remark on how wonderful I am, or any self indulging, self serving status, but to show that positives will result from the changes that you make in your life, as you start your journey to find Jesus.

Now you might be asking yourself if that is all that you need to do to change. Well, we have just started. But, the changes that we have discussed are tremendous in value, for the upcoming steps that we are to take.

Grudges

Our next step in cleansing ourselves is to stop holding onto grudges. We have to let them go. Grudges that we hold on to are really hidden anger that we have not dealt with. If we don't deal with this anger, before long, it will consume us, or it will be too late to deal with. This area worked well for me several months ago, when I learned of it from Joyce Meyers. As I read her book, I learned that I held a grudge that was deep, hidden anger for my biological father. See, I am forty-two years old, and the last time I saw him was roughly 37 years ago. However, he has always known where I have been, but on the same topic, I have always known where he has been. We have been two of the most stubborn people on the earth. While I was discussing this topic, my wife pointed out that I seemed to get worked up with a brief mention of my father. After doing some soul searching, I realized that I was bothered by this anger, and I needed to drop this anger from my life, so I took Joyce Meyers advice.

To start with, I didn't feel like talking to him because I didn't want to give him or myself the opportunity to make excuses or start telling lies. I also didn't feel we needed a relationship anymore. My father, who has raised me, would not have to share time with anybody! So, I decided to write him a letter. After a couple of attempts to write this letter, I finally got one approved by my wife. One that didn't result in hidden anger because the intent of the letter was just to drop the anger, not stir it up more. Then, I prayed over the letter and mailed it off. Once

I dropped the letter in the mailbox and rose that flag, I immediately felt better. I felt like a huge boulder had been lifted off my heart. To this day, I haven't felt any anger toward him.

Now not everyone lives that far away where a letter is the only appropriate way to deal with it. Upon arriving back to work, I felt in my interactions with others that I had some issues with a couple of people. So I decided to handle these issues in person. I started by telling these associates that I have been holding a grudge against them, and that I didn't anymore. I explained that these feeling were just realized, and I was not strong enough to handle them before. Then I asked them to forgive me for these feelings, and that I hoped that we could still be friends, or at least still have a good working relationship.

Upon clearing the air with these people, again I had these feelings of hatred and bitterness being lifted from my heart. And do you know what was crazy about one of them? One of my friends actually said that they had not noticed a problem. Sounds crazy, but the anger that I was holding on to was only hurting me and doing absolutely nothing for or against them. So what was the purpose?

What I have learned from this cleansing process is that when completed I was able to build a stronger rapport with them, that was not there before. I stopped trying to change others to fit my way of thinking, and I didn't feel like they were trying to change me anymore to fit their lifestyle.

To do this type of action requires a great deal of strength on your part, but it is worth it. What I would suggest is that before you attempt to cleanse yourself in a face-to-face encounter, that you pray first for assistance and strength to handle the encounter. For support in God's Word I suggest that you refer to the Book of Proverbs 16 verse 7, which states,

"When a man's ways please the Lord, He makes even his enemies to be at Peace with him."

If you need further clarification in this area, I also suggest that you read the complete story of Jacob and his brother Esau. This story can be found in the Book of Genesis starting in chapter 27. A brief summary showed where Jacob, the younger brother, stole Esau's birthright, and then fled the area. This caused Esau to become enraged and the threat to kill Jacob became apparent. But in the end, Jacob gave himself to the Lord, and wrestled with Him until he received a blessing from God. Jacob then met with his brother Esau, and all was forgiven. After reading this story, think about the situation from your own point of view, and ask yourself if you could wrestle with the Lord until He blessed you. The answer is easy. You certainly can, if you are sincere, if you are dependent, if you are broken and weak. It is when we are weak, that we are strong. But if we are self-righteous, if we are proud, if we are high-minded, and puffed up in our own mind, we will receive nothing from Him.

When we get down on our knees to pray, we have to find that holy place in our self. We have to find that place of meekness where we can call on God to break us down, and change, and transform us in order for Him to bless us. And in response, he will bless us exceedingly abundantly above all that we ask or think. (Ephesians 3:20)

I believe that we have covered what occurs in our mind pretty well. The battle in our mind will continue to be a battle until we take control and win. With the help of God, I believe that we can all win, and keep the devil in his place, which is out of our mind, body, and soul.

Next, we will cover some of the other vices that we have to battle. These vices are all created by the society that we live in. We see them daily on television, newscast, and movies. Society today has allowed them to dominate advertisements, and they have become more and more acceptable by standards of today. I touched on these vices earlier in my own personal example. The vices that I am referring to are the over indulgence of drinking, drugs, sexual immorality, gambling, and the use of profane language. I will address each one separately and attempt to shed further light on them in an effort to help understand these vices, so that together, with the help of God, we can win the individual battles, and conquer evil and sin first in our mind and bodies, then in all that we come in contact with.

Drinking

First we will talk about drinking. The drinking of alcoholic beverages has become socially accepted to the point that it is expected. The drinking of alcoholic beverages to the point where we lose all our inhibitions mars holidays, birthdays, and the common weekend ritual. What use to be planned events to celebrate something special, are now planned events used to drink to the point of getting drunk.

The drinking of wine is mentioned in the bible. But, what most people don't realize is that back in biblical times, it would have taken a relatively large quantity of wine for someone to lose their inhibitions. In today's advances, a single mixed beverage, or a couple of beers are enough to reduce a persons reasoning abilities.

Also, not known from biblical times, there were many places where the water sources were unreliable or contaminated. Wine filled a void, and played a crucial role as a reliable and safe source of drink to bring refreshment to a person. But, with today's advances and improved technology, we as a society have been able to purify and improve the making of an alcoholic beverage to the point where one drink is very potent.

I know and realize that we have medical experts that suggest drinking a glass of wine a day is healthy, and I don't necessarily disagree with this. However, I haven't heard or seen an advertisement that suggest that we get intoxicated to the point that we lose our thought process and place ourselves in danger, both mentally, and physically.

Basically, I am saying that the only reason that I can think of to drink to excess is that we choose to fill a personal craving from within ourselves. It is hard to accept that getting drunk is an accident. And before we choose to battle fear, loneliness, and other problematic emotions within us, we should consider the dangers associated with alcoholic beverages. Alcoholic beverages can be a destructive evil force. If we want to progress in our walk with God, we must achieve and maintain a life of purity that would separate us from the wickedness associated with the devil.

Can we find happiness without the drink? I suggest that we turn to God for help in this area. I feel that we have other avenues available to us to help fight the personal cravings that create the inner need for drunkenness. I believe that we should pray to the father, and turn to God for help with our problems. Once we have turned our problems over to Him, then we will not need to fill that void associated with drunkenness. By filling this void with God, we now have taken the chains off and are now allowed to enjoy life in a good Christian lifestyle that is very satisfying.

Drugs

Next, we will discuss the use of drugs. Now I am not talking about medicinal drugs used to cure illnesses and reduce pain and fever, but I am talking about the use of drugs that are considered illegal and the misuse of medicinal drugs. These illegal drugs and the misuse of prescription medication can and will aid in an early physical death. This precious body that has been given to you and I by God, to serve as the Temple of the Holy Spirit, we are destroying. Through the use of these products, we choose to destroy this temple, therefore, offending the Holy Spirit who helps us in our prayer to the Father.

When discussing the need for these drugs other than for medicinal purposes, we should notice that the real battle is not with people around us, but with the desires and passions that are within us.

To fight these urges to take these unnatural products, we first must turn to the Lord. We must repent for what we have already done, and believe that the Lord will help see us through. We must turn our problems over to the Lord, and allow Him to fight them for us.

Believe that this is a battle, to fight against on a daily basis. The devil has a stronghold on us when we allow these drugs to take over our lives. These drugs are used as an excuse to commit acts of violence and break the law. But, you can be cleansed and allowed freedom from this bondage. If you want to break free of these fleshy desires that the devil is using against you, you must repent, and believe the Lord is there for you. Turn to the Lord, and experience his forgiveness and his freeing power that will allow you to live you life to the fullest that it can be.

We, as a society, have to take back our lives and that of our children. We have to take a stand. We are eliminating our future by selling drugs to our children, and allowing them to sell drugs, just to make the quick, and easy money. Money that is only good for things of this flesh world.

In my own experiences being a police officer, I see the impact of drinking and drugs on the person, the family, and the community. Most of the time, the person on alcoholic beverages and drugs, are completely unaware of the damages that they have caused to themselves, and their families. The mind-altering affects that these products have on us, is unbelievable. Most of the time, these people promise never to do this again, and beg for help in their moment of need. However, most refuse in the end to ask for assistance from God. Most think they are strong enough personally to handle the change. Unfortunately, they don't realize that they were not strong enough to stay away from these problems to begin with. So the cycle remains in tact.

Sex

Next we will discuss the areas of sex in our society. Sex is regarded as the highest form of intimacy between a man and women, who have committed themselves to each other. However this intimate act has been made trivial, like a game played or a sport. It seems like we are trying to have the most partners, and other goals that take away from the intimacy and special connection that is created. To place it another way, sex use to be like having a piece of chocolate cake, increasingly satisfying, due to the enriched taste that was experienced ever so often. But now, sex is like drinking water. It has been diluted in today's society. For those who still have that special intimacy, I salute you.

The Bible presents sex as a gift from God. However, the topic of sex has often been something not to talk about, even though the Bible has been quite open about it. The Bible presents sex as something sacred that occurs between a man and a woman. It is described as something holy when the two bodies become one flesh, committed to each other as it occurs within God's plan.

In reference to marriage, the Bible reflects that all should honor the bond of marriage, and the marriage bed should be kept pure. (Supported in Hebrews 13:4) This passage describes how not only should the partners in the marriage have rules to abide by, but also everyone has rules to abide by as it comes to marriage, and that sacred vow that has been taken in front of God.

Do you know that there is great percentage of domestic violence problems in the world, due to violating, or the thought of violating this specific rule about the sacred bond of marriage? The violation of this rule has caused divorce, the separation of children, broken bones, mental incapacity, and even death. Sex and the vows of marriage are important. So much so that lives have been lost, and fell into the pit of hell for eternity due to a few minutes of pleasure that violated a very simple rule. I'll leave you to think of any questions that you have further on this topic, and how it can create a major change in your life, depending on what decision you might make on this subject.

Gambling

Gambling has been described to possess something of another, which usually is money. When we gamble we create a risk of our own, to attempt through chance to gain the possessions of another with nothing to give in exchange. Gambling has become center stage for a lot of people. Think about it, just a couple of years ago, the only place to play cards and gamble on other casino games, was at a casino. Now with the acceptance of gambling, you can play every minute of everyday, year round with the assistance of the Internet.

Now you might ask, why is gambling wrong? Well, when one person wins either in a card game, a casino game, or even the lottery, that person only won, due to the loss of another. Gambling is categorized as stealing by consent.

Gambling is a violation of the three most honorable ways of exchanging money. When referring to the Bible, we find that the law of labor is the most common way of achieving the financial gains necessary. This is where we earn money for an expected labor that we have provided. Secondly, we find the law of exchange. This is where we exchange one thing for money or something of equal value. And thirdly we find the law of love. This is very uncommon in today's society. This is the expression of love for mankind through Christ by the gift of money or something of value, without the expectation of receiving something in return.

When referring to God's Word about work, let us look at the Book of Ephesians 4:28, which states,

"Let him who stole steal no longer, but rather let him labor, working with his hands what is good, that he may have something to give him who has need."

As you ponder these three laws, and try to see how they would affect you life, remember that work is honorable for Christians, and gambling harms our resources, and for the most part, leaves us broke and in such a need that the devil can get a stronghold on us, which in turn could create the committing of crimes to replace such things lost.

Profane Language

What do I mean by profane language? This is the swearing, cussing, and additional insults that we in society use to express ourselves in a nasty way in an effort usually to protect ourselves from attack from others, or utilized in such a way to fit into the group, sounding big and bad, and cool. But when we refer to the scripture of the Bible found in the Book of Matthew 5:34-35, it states,

> *"But I say to you, do not swear at all: neither by heaven, for it is God's Throne; nor by the earth, for it is His footstool; nor by Jerusalem, for it is the city of the Great King."*

As you reflect on these passages, try to think about why cussing and swearing has become so commonly accepted and used in society today. What use to be rated "R" in the theaters and on television, now has been reduced to "PG-13", and can be seen on the television daily.

Some people have stated that the act of swearing is personally gratifying. These people have stated that because the act of swearing fits into the conversation to show the emotion of the conversation, therefore, it was needed. However, I would go to state that there is no pleasure in using profane language, because it produces no personal satisfaction, nor does it really result in the receiver changing their operating status.

Going beyond personal satisfaction, it also goes against God's Word. The act of swearing is heinous in God's sight. It is not needed. The only result in swearing is that the receiver takes offense to the commission of this act, and it hardens their heart, and usually builds a grudge between two or more people of God.

For further understanding, coming from the Book of Matthew 15:17-18, Jesus said,

"Do you not yet understand that whatever enters the mouth goes into the stomach and is eliminated? But those things which proceed out of the mouth come from the heart, and they defile a man."

So, the next time we go to speak, let us pause for just a moment, and think before we speak. Emotions sometimes run wild, but that is no excuse. We all have had enough education and training from our family and friends, through television, and schools, to know that we are able to communicate effectively without the use of such vulgar and filthy language. The next time you feel the desire to curse, refer to God's Word and find something else to satisfy that craving. The Bible is full of such insightful and pleasurable remarks that the use of would only make you strive to become better.

The purpose of this chapter has been to open your minds and your heart to see where the devil has been afforded an opportunity to get a foot into your heart, mind, and eventually soul. Being a police officer, I see bad things like this that have effected whole families, and torn them apart. As a person, formerly taking into some of these acts, I can speak from first hand knowledge that these acts can and potentially will tear holes into relationships and families that are hard to fix. In conclusion, take what I have said and take it to heart. Change now while you still have the chance. Turn to the Lord, pray to Him, and ask Him for help. I know that you will find Him as a great source of power, and strength.

<u>Chapter Four</u>

New Rationale of Thinking

◈

Now that we have made some specific changes in our lives that will help nurture and strengthen our relationship with God, let us talk about this new rationale of thinking, and how this new thought process changes how we handle everyday activity. Once we accepted Jesus Christ as our savior, we are able to receive the mindset of Christ. This allows us to start a fresh and a new. Now, we will look at things differently. What use to be opportunities to cut someone down, or poke fun at, become opportunities to witness to and share our new beliefs and desires.

As we start our journey in this new lifestyle, taking these brand new steps down the path, we will be striving to obtain the "Fruits of the Holy Spirit." Once we obtain the "Fruits of the Holy Spirit" then we can obtain the "Gifts of the Holy Spirit." What we have to remember is that there is no set time-line for achieving these steps. All that we can do is accept God's timing in these matters, and do our very best to walk in the path that He has laid before us. God's plan for each of us is awesome, and can't be rushed. As we wait to achieve the many steps in God's Will for us, we can live in the joy and comfort of His love, while witnessing to others as we try to lead by example, in this new lifestyle, of our Christian Walk with God.

New Thought Process

When we give our body, mind, and soul to the Lord, we are saved, and, we receive the Mind of Christ. This new mindset allows us to start a fresh, new lifestyle. When looking for support through God's Word, we should review Ephesians Chapter 4 verses 17-24, again. We should start to appreciate the life God has given us, the opportunity of an everlasting life with Him, and to believe that the truth of all things lies in Jesus. We should start to adapt our life and live it in the holy and righteous state that it was meant to be in. We should seek honesty and rely on telling the truth at all times.

When doing this, we will find that we will want to start having an honest living, while helping the needy and the poor. When we speak, it will generally be associated with helpful, and encouraging words. And when placed in the position of power or judgment, we will find that we have more compassion and forgiveness toward others, who may have crossed us or hampered us in our new way of living.

Being a supervisor in the police arena, I found that when someone made a mistake that in my opinion was kind of trivial; I had more compassion than before. What use to be, "policy states" now was basically an opportunity to train someone for the better. Instead of hammering someone with punishment through punitive discipline, now was a chance to address problems and help someone through corrective action.

For those of you who don't know the difference, punitive discipline is a hard sheet of paper that is placed in your permanent personnel file, attached with potentially days off without pay. Where as, corrective action, is looked upon as a minor infraction that required some remedial training, and resulted in a sheet of paper that is showed in your shift supervisors file, and a training sheet of paper that showed in your permanent personnel file.

This new thought process now had ridden such bad emotions of envy, hate, jealousy, and anger and are filled with other positive emotions that deal with helping people both in the ranks and the citizens of the community.

This new thought process injected positive emotion in my thinking. I was able to avoid negative emotions, and avoid not caring about my fellow man, because it is the negative emotions that trap us into regressing. Regressing is classified as backsliding. And backsliding is noted as a condition that requires divine healing. (Supported by Jeremiah 3:22) And in my spiritual walk with God, I don't want to take any steps backwards if I can help it.

But, if by some chance that you do regress, get into your prayer closet, hit your knees immediately and pray to the Lord for your healing. Repent openly to God, and allow Him to make the changes in you that are necessary.

Fruits of the Spirit

I start off this area of concern with a quote in scripture, taken from the Book of Galatians 5:22-23, where it states,

> *"But the fruit of the Spirit is love, joy, peace, long-suffering, kindness, goodness, faithfulness, gentleness, self-control. Against such there is no law."*

The first three, Love, Joy, and Peace, concern our own personal attitude. The second three, Longsuffering,

Kindness, and Goodness, deals with social relationships, and the third three, Faithfulness, Gentleness, and Self-control, deal with our conduct as Christians.

If you will think about these Fruits of the Holy Spirit, you will notice that none of them are self-serving. There are no fruits that fall in line with the passions and desires of the seven deadly sins. To put it another way, the Fruits of the Holy Spirit do not serve the passions and desires of this world, as we know it now. They lead us to something better. They lead us to the Kingdom of God a place far better than this world has to offer.

In interpreting the Fruits of the Holy Spirit, you and I have to understand what they are, and incorporate them into our daily life. Once you and I have the chance to understand these Fruits of the Holy Spirit better, and as we incorporate them into our lives, more and more, then we will be better off to receive the Gifts of the Holy Spirit.

If you wish to incorporate these fruits into your life, I encourage you to take the necessary steps to make these changes immediately. When you set out on your day, take a couple of these fruits with you. As you interact with people in person, and even on the phone, work diligently to incorporate these fruits into your thought process. Make them a part of your mindset. I think that as you use them in your everyday life they will become more and more part of your nature, and the reactions that you will receive will be positive re-enforcement for your journey.

As you mature in your steps to become more Christ-like, the Holy Spirit will develop these Fruits of the Holy Spirit in our lives. This happens as we continue to live our lives completely for Jesus.

Gifts of the Holy Spirit

The Gifts of the Holy Spirit are different than the Fruits of the Holy Spirit. Where as the Fruits are within you changing how you act and respond to things daily in your life, the Gifts are utilized to give praise and worship to God, and to edify the Church. Again, there is no self-serving in these Gifts, just like the Fruits of the Holy Spirit.

When referencing the Gifts of the Holy Spirit, I advise you to look them up and read them yourself. You can find them in the Bible, in the Book of 1 Corinthians Chapter 12 verses 8-10. You will find that there are nine Gifts that the Holy Spirit helps you to utilize in your daily walk with God. These nine Gifts are as follows:

1) *The Word of Wisdom*
2) *The Word of Knowledge*
3) *Faith*
4) *The Gifts of Healing*
5) *The Working of Miracles*
6) *Prophecy*
7) *The Discernment of Spirits*
8) *Speaking in Different Kinds of Tongues*
9) *Interpretation of Tongues*

Now I could attempt to explain each Gift separately, however, that would take another book to explain. So do some research for yourself and get to know exactly what these Gifts are. Once you understand what they are, pray to God for only the very best of them for you. God knows you, and knows what you are capable of. He will choose which to give you, based on what He believes that you can handle.

Once you receive the Gift(s) from God, remember to incorporate them daily into your life, but not for personal gain, only in the praising and worshipping of God, and edifying the Church.

When receiving the Gift(s) of the Holy Spirit, remember that once you receive this Gift or Gifts, that you increase in responsibility to the Lord, the church, and the people around you. As in material things of the fleshy world, there is responsibility assigned to you when you receive this Gift for the Holy Spirit.

Changing Lifestyles

Once you start handling yourself in this new rationale of thinking, you will notice things from the past that you wish you could change. At least I have. The first thing that I have noticed is that changing people and accepting people as they are has not always been my creed. There is a very fine line on how to handle these situation, because who are you and I to judge people and change them to our own specification.

I will give you a couple of examples to go by. One example deals with what turned out to be a good change, and the second, a change that has affected my interaction with my wife. I won't say that this change was a good or bad change, just that due to my stubbornness, a change has occurred in my wife, a sacrifice if you will, that has taken some enjoyment from her. But let us start.

My first example starts with my wife urging me to attend church. The attention my wife placed on attending church was always in a positive way, however, it required some sacrifice on my part, therefore, became hard to accomplish. But, as time went on, I started to attend, with my wife, and children. And, of course, this change resulted in a very positive change in me personally, and in the lifestyle that I live.

I use to think that my work schedule wouldn't allow me to attend church on a regular basis, but I started to find that I was looking for more reasons, and more opportunities to attend church. The feelings and excitement that I received from church, changed how I looked at things happening in my life. The tingly feeling that I would receive from attending church, transformed me into a praising warrior for the Lord. I started reading more and more books, and singing more and more in my patrol car, that to by passers, I must have looked like a fool. But, who cares how I looked, I was praising God, nothing else mattered. Was this a change for the better? You bet it was, and a change that I will appreciate for the rest of my life.

If you don't go to church now, maybe it is something that you need to try. And if you go to church now, and don't understand what I am talking about or experiencing, then maybe you are going to the wrong church. Now, I am not trying to tell you that some churches are wrong in what they do. What I am trying to tell you is that some churches are not alive in the way they preach the message, and get the point across of God's Word. What I suggest is that you find the church that works for you. Find the church that expresses God's Love, in a manner that you can recognize and that moves within you. Where the first church you attend might seem slow or even boring, there is another out there that will strike a cord within you, and will motivate you into becoming all that you can be in God's infinite plan.

Now the next example is a little different. My wife likes to dance. That's just not my cup of tea. But, my wife likes to dance and enjoy life like that. She enjoys the occasional going to a club and dancing for an hour or two. However, I refused to go. Either we didn't have the money, didn't have the time, or this wasn't the thing that a supervisor with the police department was suppose to do. Well, now I have won this battle. Shouldn't I be happy? Well, I'm not. I have changed my wife. I have changed the person that she was, into the person that she is today, giving up something that she enjoyed to do. Something that didn't hurt anyone, or anybody, that only gave her a chance to reduce stress and tension from the job, and provide just a few minutes of enjoyment. Now this, of course, doesn't revolve around the Bible, or worshipping God, but provides an example of how we can change people, just by refusing to give in to their needs, instead of our own. Now, I have to make up for this, sounds like I'm going dancing soon, so I can tell her, "I'm sorry."

By these examples you can tell that sometimes things change for the positive, and sometimes not. The question comes up though as to who are we to try to make changes in other people. Are we trained enough to be able to make these kinds of decisions? I think not!

These examples are given to show that how we handle ourselves, and how we interact with others can change people without being conscious of what and how we are doing this. Now if we were to start to live our lives with the Fruits of the Holy Spirit, wouldn't our ability to change other people, even if it were not our intent, were for the better. At least it would be based on very positive, good emotions, and not based on personal motives, and negative emotions.

When referring to the Bible, looking in the Book of Matthew Chapter 6 verse 33 and Jesus said,

"But seek first the Kingdom of God and His righteousness, and all these things shall be added to you."

This scripture shows that we should not be preoccupied with material things of this earth; our attention should be to seek God's kingdom and righteousness. And we should know that as we do this, God would add all these things to us. This is the covenant of faithfulness that the Lord will respond, as long as we seek Him. But we have to get right in ourselves first before the Lord will provide. We have to be earnest and sincere.

As I was searching and seeking God, I questioned for a while why I hadn't received the Gifts of the Holy Spirit? As I searched and prayed, I found the answer. I had received my answer to my prayers. As we start our journey seeking the Lord, we sometimes forget that the Lord acts as our Father. Now how many times have your parents gave you everything you have ever wanted. It just doesn't happen. Well, the same thing occurs with God. God can see in our hearts and in our minds, and knows more about us than we know. God finds out if we are ready for the gifts and whether we can handle the gifts with great responsibility. Fortunately, God sometimes answers prayers with...NO! Sometimes, the answer is not yet! But these are answers.

We should put God's kingdom first in our lives. This is the first step on the pathway to where we can learn to determine His will, purpose, and call for our life. We should turn toward God's Word. This is the pathway to understanding his will for us. As we do this, we should learn to recognize His way as we hear the voice of His spirit as it directs us.

Once we receive the Baptism of the Holy Ghost, then that opens the door to having the Gifts of the Holy Spirit! As these changes occur, we won't have to worry about changing people anymore. See we don't change people ourselves, we introduce them to Jesus, and Jesus changes them. And these changes that Jesus makes are always for the better.

So, what keeps us away from the spiritual gifts that we so desire? We have to improve in ourselves. In an effort to get these spiritual gifts, we have to achieve the fruits of spirit. By consciously using these Fruits of the Spirit in our daily life, we will achieve great steps toward receiving the Gifts of the Holy Spirit.

So, when we hit our knees and pray to the Lord, when we ask for the spiritual gifts that we all want so badly, remember to first ask for the fruits of the spirit. Just like when we eat dinner with our family, our Father doesn't want us to have dessert before we have the main course.

As in all things, when trying to find the answers, turn to God. Seek first Him. Find your prayer closet, and hit your knees. Search that place of meekness within you, and pray to Him. The more you turn your problems over to Him, you will find that your problems are minor in appearance, and that in a short amount of time, they are over, as the Lord deals with it in His time.

Seek the Lord first, and turn your problems over to Him. THE BATTLE IS THE LORD'S, NOT YOURS.

Chapter Five

Spiritual Steps to Achieve

Traditionally, when we build, whether it is a house, a relationship, or an education, we must first start with the laying of cornerstones. Cornerstones are the buildings foundation. Cornerstones are the essential character traits that are developed and nurtured by a personal relationship with Jesus Christ.

Going straight to the Bible for insight, we find in the Book of Acts 2:42-47, that the author is telling us about how to grow as a person of the spirit. To put it in to an example for today's society, imagine an athlete, whether professional or even in the local high schools today. They practice daily on building muscle mass, developing strength, and making their bodies the best that it can be. What can we do to exercise our spiritual muscle, and train the generations to follow? Well, we have to first start with believing that Jesus Christ came in the flesh. We have to accept that he is our Lord and Savior. Then we have to study the word. Study God's beautiful and powerful, life filled word. During our studies, we have to fellowship and pray to the Lord for assistance. We have to care for others, and love the Lord, through praise and worship to him, while witnessing to others for him.

Now there are a lot of books covering religion out there. Regular books are designed for entertainment and education. But we have to be careful of what we take in to our mind, and our heart. When we read books on religion, we have to understand that a mortal human being writes most books. And we already know that human beings are capable of mistakes. Some of the authors that I have read, and have faith in are Benny Hinn, Joyce Meyers, Charles and Frances Hunter, Lt. Col. Shaw Clifton, as well as works by, Smith Wigglesworth, Lester Sumrall, and John G. Lake. But we have to remember that regular books feed the mind. But the book we need to concentrate on, feeds the heart and soul. That book that I am speaking about is not really a book. It is like an oxygen bottle for those who can't breath, a pacemaker for those whose heart will not beat, crutches for those who can't walk, and a sword for those who must fight. The book that I am referring to is, of course, the Bible. The Bible is not just a book...it is life. And if you want to spiritually live, and be all that you can be, you must ingest this knowledge with your whole soul.

The Bible

So first, we should start to read the Bible. The Bible is a big book, so don't pick one up and get distraught thinking either it's too much, or the words don't make any sense. Be smart in the study guide that you choose. First you have to get the appropriate Bible for your ability to understand. Unless you have been to seminary school, or some other special training, some Bibles are hard to understand. I choose the New Spirit Filled Life Bible, New King James Version put out by Thomas Nelson Bibles. In this Bible they have commentary at the bottom of the pages, plus Truth in Action pages at the conclusion of each chapter to assist with further clarification. However, do your research well, and pick the right Bible for you. There are many out there. If you have questions, ask your local pastor, or a Christian friend for assistance. You will find that the pastor has a wealth of information to assist you, and your Christian friend will go out of his or her way to assist you.

When you have settled on the appropriate Book of Life for you, you have to choose where to start. Some people say, start with chapter one and go till you finish. Some say other things. I started with the Book of Revelations, because that was the message in Church that day. Now let me tell you, that was a mistake. So don't start there. But, to provide assistance, I suggest that you start with the gospels of the New Testament. Start with Matthew, Mark, Luke, and John. This will give you a great foundation to build on. Or, if you asked for assistance, check with them for a suggestion as to where to start. This provides an equal basis for you and them to share. And in this action, they can kind of act like a mentor to you, while you start your spiritual journey.

Now when you start to read the Bible, choose to read it everyday. You don't have to finish a whole chapter a day. But read until you become tired. When you realize that you mind is becoming fatigued, find a place to stop, because you aren't really doing yourself any good, if your mind isn't there with you. Now when you find a place to read the Bible, choose a place that offers you some quality alone time. In front of the television, with the Super Bowl playing isn't going to offer you a bit of help. Find a place where you can concentrate on what you read. Then pray. Yes, pray. Pray to the Lord for assistance in your journey. Ask the Lord to allow the Holy Spirit, that rest within you, to open up the word to you for complete understanding. Once you have finished your prayers, start to read, and enjoy God's blessed word. As you read, pause occasionally and think about what you have read, and does it apply to your life in any way. Of course, I am relying on you to be honest with yourself. Remember, only you and the good Lord know what you are thinking. While reading the Bible, lying to yourself is only fighting the urge to learn.

If you come across areas where you are lost, ask your mentor for assistance. If it is late at night, or your mentor is unavailable, check the Internet for references. There are plenty of good resources out there. Take for example www.bluebible.org, or www.blueletterbible.org just to name a couple. These are good references when you don't have assistance elsewhere. Plus there are commentaries listed that allow you to read the Word in more common language. And if you get really interested in your studies, then you can purchase programs to load on your computer, such as Bible Explorer, that will allow you to study out scriptures like you were actually going to minister in church.

Once you start reading God's Word more frequently, upon completion every night, get back down and pray. Pray to the Lord, thanking him for His Word, and anything that it might have meant to you on that given day. You can never fellowship with God too much. He longs for it, and as you prosper in your studies, you will find that you desire it more. These prayers can be powerful, but we will speak more on prayer a little later in this chapter.

Training Our Children

Next, to press forward in our journey, we should train our children, and our families around us. The love that we have gained for the Lord now flows from us and has to go somewhere. Why not share it with the ones that we love? It is mentioned in the Bible, in the Book of Judges 2:10, where is states,

> *"When all that generation had been gathered to their fathers, another generation arose after them who did not know the Lord not the work which He had done for Israel."*

So what does this mean? Well, it shows that we are supposed to train up our families and children. If we wait till later, we might run out of time. If we don't train these people up now, when it is their turn to lead, how will they lead, without the knowledge, and love of the Lord, if they never knew of it? In the scriptures it shows that when the leader passed away, Joshua at this time, the children of Israel did not remember the Lord their God, who had delivered them from the hands of all their enemies. During their rebellion from God, they were oppressed, impoverished, enslaved, and plundered by their enemies. When they turned back to the Lord, they experienced deliverance, restoration, freedom, and victory. God calls to us today to pursue him and to walk in his ways, to realize his purpose and blessing. So mentor to the next generation to know and trust God. Teach them of His marvelous works so that they might grow up to serve and follow Him faithfully.

When training your families and friends, remember that it starts with their ability to see the Christian lifestyle at work in your life. When they notice how you handle yourself in public and in private, they will see the love and mercy that you show. When you go to mentor to them, they will be much more receptive to your attempts because they already understand that you walk what you preach. Therefore, they won't fear deceit from you.

Now I believe that we should start sharing and teaching our children. The difference between a child and the wise and prudent person is this. The wise man knows too much, therefore, it clouds his mind. The prudent person is too careful in his actions to be able to follow with all his heart. But children are different. They eagerly receive.

When our children were babies, they were sometimes so ravenous that we had to pull the bottle back from them, or they would swallow the whole bottle of milk, taking it in too fast. So by this very action alone, it shows that children are eager to take in all that they can.

So when we share this spiritual knowledge, we develop a working structure that can add support to all that we do. This is a working structure that will allow us to help each other in the times of crisis, and allows us to not be alone, but as a group of knowledgeable soldiers in God's Army. And I'll explain my thoughts on God's Army later in this book.

What else do we accomplish? We instill in our children confidence, knowledge, and wisdom, while God equips them up to be powerful in the Word of God. Plus it is a better foundation for your children, to help them achieve their own goals that they have. In the Book of Proverbs 22:6, it states,

"Train up a child in the way he should go, and when he is old he will not depart from it."

Now is the time to build a strong foundation in our children, a foundation that will keep them in check when they are out in the real world, away from their families and friends.

Next to personally knowing Jesus and walking with him, one of the greatest blessings of the Christian life is to actually lead someone to Jesus Christ. Why not start with our own children, our family, and our friends. The good news is that God wants to use us as an instrument to speak to others. Jesus gave us this commission in the Book of Mark 16:15-16 where he states,

> *And He said to them, "Go into all the world and preach the gospel to every creature. He who believes and is baptized will be saved; but he who does not believe will be condemned."*

This wonderful charge is known as the great commission; however, it seems to be interpreted by so many as the great suggestion. Can you see anything in that scripture that leads us to believe this is merely a suggestion? A suggestion that we can take and decide for ourselves whether it is right or not. Isn't this how Israel regressed into so much trouble, in the past.

So how do we accomplish this feat? We have to start training our families and friends. Once we accept this role, we will see that we can avoid the reoccurring problem of humanity losing contact with the Lord, and his teachings. So, we should develop our children, who are our future. That is our future, until Jesus comes back for you and me.

Fasting

Fasting by pure definition is the act of willingly abstaining from some or all food and in some cases drink for a period of time. Fasting for religious and spiritual reasons has been a part of human custom for a long time. Fasting is mentioned in the Bible, in both the Old and New Testaments.

I know, it sounds hard, and you know what, it is, at least at first. But remember that there are all kinds of fasts that are offered to the Lord. The important thing to remember is to let God know what you are doing as a gift for Him, and let Him know what it is you are seeking. When you start, confess your sins to God, and ask the Holy Spirit to show you areas of weakness that you need help in. Forgive all in your heart that have offended you, and ask for forgiveness from others that you may have offended. Surrender your life fully to Jesus Christ, and reject the worldly desires and passions that tempt you during this time. And remember to let God know what it is you are seeking, whether it is guidance, peace, rest, protection, or whatever.

When you start fasting, try something that you can do or handle, but is still a challenge. In the Book of Esther, it shows where she fasted for three days without food, and only drank water. Did it work? Of course it did. She fasted in an effort to save a nation. In the Book of Daniel, it shows where Daniel fasted for twenty-one days eating only vegetables. That is no meat, and no bread for twenty-one days. It sounds pretty easy doesn't it, but after a week or two, it becomes pretty hard.

When you are trying to decide which kind of fast to participate in, ask the Holy Spirit for guidance. If you want to do the full fast for multiply days, and after three days don't think you are strong enough to continue, change to the Daniel's fast, and complete more days of glorious giving to the Lord. Completing a combination of fasts is alright. The fast itself is an act of giving something up for the Lord. He will know what you are doing for Him.

Besides the normal going without eating, what is fasting? To answer that question, I refer to the Book of Matthew 6:16-18, where it states,

"Moreover, when you fast, do not be like the hypocrites, with a sad countenance. For they disfigure their faces that they may appear to men to be fasting. Assuredly, I say to you, they have their reward. But for you, when you fast, anoint your head and wash your face, so that you do not appear to men to be fasting, but to your Father who is in the secret place; and your Father who sees in secret will reward you openly."

Simply put, fasting is an outward indication of your inward sincerity. Fasting is also when you want to show God that you are sincere in your repentance of your sins. These verses also tell us that we are not to gripe about our fasting and make it overly known what we are doing. The fast is something only shared with God. That's a portion of it that makes it so personal to the Lord. Now I am not saying that if you are participating in a group fast, that you can't talk to the other participants about it. That would be ridiculous. However, to bring fasting into proper perspective, it is better to be lean and hurting in the body, while your soul prospers, rather than being wasted away in the soul, while your body enjoys the feast.

When you start fasting, start with a clear goal, about why you are fasting, and what you hope to accomplish. Ask the Holy Spirit for guidance before, and during your fast. During your fast remember to pray more, especially during the times you are giving something up to the Lord, and read the Bible.

Is it only for believers? No, because in the Book of Daniel it also shows where the wicked King Darius fasted to God, and the Lord reached him. Showing that if we fear God, and walk according to the righteous path, we will receive peace. King Darius did, and so can you.

During your fasting, remember to add prayer and a daily amount of God's Word to your fasting. While you are seeking God's assistance, add prayer to fellowship with Him, as well as reading the Bible. I think that you will find that He will listen, and His word will start to reveal more and more to you.

Lastly, remember to check with your medical doctor about any kind of medical issues that you might have, to ensure that you chose the appropriate fast. While on the fast, remember to take your medication and vitamins. Pick a fast that is right for you. I don't like to let my children fast, at least for very long. I encourage them to do away with television or video games for the specified period of time. This is considered a fast of sacrifice. The purpose of the fast is to graciously give to the Lord what it is we give up. To put it in another way, each meal given up is presented to God, in front of His Thrown, as a gift, a memorial.

When your fast is over, don't jump in an over eat to start with. When I came off the first fast that I ever participated in, I ate a large pepperoni pizza, and a hoagie sub sandwich. My body thought that I had lost my mind. And, of course, my body got me back. But, when you come off your fast, begin eating solid foods gradually, and in smaller portions, which will allow your body to become more accustomed to food again.

Prayer

We should pray at all times. There are no limitations to when we should pray. That's why we should pray when we wake, when we eat, before we go to sleep, and anytime we actually think about it. When the thought of prayer comes into our mind, how do you think it got in there? Luckily for us, God's Word provides, and teaches us the art of praying. When we look in the Book of Luke 11:1-13, we find that God has left us the path to finding Him thru prayer. Just remember that when you pray, do so with a pure and sincere heart.

When we pray, we will receive power to make it over the next hurdle that be fronts us. We will receive peace and tranquility that was so apparent in the flesh life that Jesus Christ demonstrated. While reading the New Testament, you'll notice that Jesus often took time to pray and fellowship with the Father. If Jesus prayed often, then how often should we?

In the Book of James 5:15-16, it states,

"And the prayer of faith will save the sick, and the Lord will raise him up. And if he has committed sins, he will be forgiven. Confess your trespasses to one another, and pray for one another, that you may be healed. The effective fervent prayer of a righteous man avail much."

When we pray, we must be persistent in our prayers, using a sense of boldness and urgency. We must show that we are earnest and wholehearted in our prayers. God has given us his Holy Spirit to aid us in our prayers. And the Holy Spirit will even assist us, when we don't know what to pray for.

Now when we pray, we need to get to a place where we can concentrate with no distractions. Remember the examples given when we started to read our Bibles. When we pray, we shouldn't have the television going, or the radio blasting. We need to give it our full attention. Our fellowship with the Father deserves our full attention.

I have talked mostly about our personal prayer time. There are other types of prayer that you should enlist to as well, however, I believe that we need to learn how to pray by ourselves, for ourselves, and others. If you have a prayer group at you local church, you can request that they add you to their prayers. I believe that you will find that they would be happy to accommodate you. You can also visit the altar call at the end of the church service, where you can be anointed with oil, and prayed for with the laying of hands by your pastor. This kind of prayer is awesome. I often find that there is an energy that flows throughout the whole prayer session that makes me feel alive, and pumped.

Just remember though, prayer is nothing without a sincere heart and pure faith in your beliefs. If you pray because that's what somebody said to do, and you are hesitant, you are wasting your time. Seek personal assistance from your pastor, or a Christian friend that can help clear your mind of the obstacles that block your path to the heavenly Father.

You and I are nothing without Him; we are absolutely dependant upon Him. I am absolutely nothing without the power and anointing of the Holy Spirit. It is through a life of dependence that there is a life of power. If you are not there, get alone with God. Seek Him diligently, and be persistent in your request to achieve this fellowship with Him.

Chapter Six

Pressing Forward

To break this world down into simple examples, there are two entities involved in the control of the people of the earth. One entity is here to take people of the earth by force. To devour them in any way he can. He tells lies, and spreads false hopes to all the people of the earth. He lives on the fear of the people, and gains power from negative emotions that he stirs up. He attacks through the man made seven deadly sins, to encourage mankind to give up on everything good and loving of the second entity.

The other entity wants to have control over the people of the earth as well, however, He will not impose Himself upon us, He waits on us to make a decision, based on all the facts and circumstances surrounding His word. He has given His only begotten son to cleanse His people of all sin and disease. And He tells only the truth, because it is impossible for Him to lie.

The first entity has no control over the other, yet he is forceful at all times, and cheats and steals. The second has power over the first, yet He doesn't use it, because He wants the people of the earth to have a choice. He doesn't want anyone that doesn't want to be with Him.

The first entity is the devil. He and his group of people will do anything to improve his numbers and strengthen his position of power. The second entity is, of course, God. Who does He have fighting for Him? Well, He has us. We are standing on that wall for Him.

Now the earth is covered with three different types of people. The first group, has already chose to stay loyal to the first entity. The second group has chose to be loyal to the second entity. And the third group hasn't chosen anyone. They are involved in the things of the flesh and are busy little bees without a care in the world about what will happen when their flesh life is over.

The first group gets the benefit of being able to burn in hell for eternity. Dealing with an eternity of pain and suffering. The second group gets the luxury of being able to walk in the kingdom of heaven for eternity. Where do you think the third group will end up? Well, they don't have either the first or second entity chasing them. The first entity doesn't have to chase, he gets them if nothing changes in them. If they stay as is in their world of flesh, chasing the fleshy worlds dream of materialistic things, and being oblivious to their God given rights of choice for their eternal soul, then the first entity wins. The second entity will not impose upon their free will. He only wants those who freely and voluntarily want to be with Him. However, He does grieve that they don't know or realize the truth about Him. So the only people who chase this group are the people of the second entity. They are considered the free agents if you will. They are free to choose to give their life to God, or reject His offer and end up in the pit with the devil. This is where we come into play. Even though it is their choice to make, that doesn't mean that they know all the facts and circumstances about how truly important their decision is. So we have to get out there and shake the bushes. We have to get out there and spread the word. God is not going to impose upon anyone, without being invited. So it is up to us to fill His kingdom, and take free labor of our brothers and sisters away from the devil.

Now we have to go out and live how we preach. We are now more familiar with what to say to people, and how to deal with people. But, now we have to go out and walk the walk, especially if we are going to talk the talk.

Where do we start? I believe that we have to start with witnessing. We have to start witnessing, because it is a part of our life. We need to express what we have learned through our research and studies, communicate what we have learned, and how we handle ourselves in public, as well as private. If we choose not to witness, then how are we to spread God's Word? If we choose not to act as Christian are suppose to act, then how will anybody take us seriously?

There won't be a whole lot of subcategories in this chapter, because they all tie in together. The steps involved in this will be useful in all your witnessing efforts. I believe that we have to witness to our children, family, and friends. Then, we need to provide some testimony to the church. This can be as easy as just asking the pastor if you could have some time to provide some personal testimony. This will demonstrate your intentions in the church, plus provide you with a foundation to ask your pastor, or an elder of the church to act as your mentor. Then, we should witness in public. Once we have achieved all three areas of witnessing, giving your own personal testimony, as well as, Jesus Christ's story will become easier. But, remember that the Christian walk is not just about what we say, and when we say it. It also encompasses how people interpret our lifestyle through our attitudes, how we handle ourselves both in the calm and the storm.

I believe that we should start with our own family. What better way to start your Christian walk than by expressing yourself to your family, and helping them get into the Kingdom of Heaven, as well. Besides isn't witnessing to our family part of the rules of God. In the Book of Proverbs 22:6, it states,

"Train up a child in the way he should go, and when he is old he will not depart from it."

Next to personally knowing Jesus and walking with Him, one of the greatest blessings of the Christian life is to actually lead someone to Jesus Christ. Why not start with our own children, family, and friends. The good news is that God wants to use us as an instrument to speak to others. Jesus gave us what is known as "The Great Commission" in the Book of Mark 16:15.

In the Book of Mark 16:15, it states,

"Go into all the world and preach the gospel to every creature."

This wonderful charge, or order, was given by Jesus Christ, but unfortunately so many people have interpreted this mighty message as "The Great Suggestion." Can someone tell me when God's word became a suggestion? A suggestion that we can take and decide for ourselves whether it is right or not. In reading the Old Testament, I think that you will find that Israel regressed into so much trouble, so many times, because they failed to adhere to this simple rule. Every time a leader, who was clear on God's word, passed away, there was no one to take his place, to lead, and to stay true to God's word.

Now I believe that we have to start sharing and teaching our children in God's word. Our children are sponges, willingly accepting the truth. Take for example my six-year-old girl. She has just learned to read. So she diligently reads almost every day. She reads just about a different book every day. She has taken to this new ability to the point that her teacher has asked that we get her to decrease her reading time, as to not get too far ahead of her classmates.

Now, what would happen if children developed that same passion for God, His teachings, and the ministering of His word? I believe that there is no limit to what children can do, because a child has not been trained by the flesh world to know or accept limitations, and to become fearful of prejudice and mockery.

To achieve this mission, your steps are not difficult, however, they mean so much. You don't need any special training to share the message of the Lord. A changed heart is all you need to begin sharing your faith with others. (Supported by John 9:1-41) One of the biggest reasons many Christians haven't shared their faith is that they feel God could never use them to draw people to Himself. Even if you don't feel qualified, once you allowed Jesus Christ into your life as your Lord and savior, you can begin to tell others of your newfound faith.

Some of the finer points of witnessing to your family is that you have to be open to God's leading, such as having a willing heart. You must share the message of the gospels, because it is the story of life, death, and the resurrection of Jesus Christ. And, you must be willing to share you own personal story with them. You should never underestimate the strength of your own story. Every believer has a testimony. Some may be more dramatic than others, however, your own story will help you find common ground with the non-believer. When they see that you are a normal person, just like them, who has had trials, just like them, then they might be open to what you have to say.

We must show in our lives that God is at work in our hearts. God desires that we demonstrate our spiritual growth through outward actions. We must live out our faith. Faith without deeds is incomplete. God saved us for a purpose. While God himself gave us salvation, he planned that our salvation would lead to good works. And our walk should match our talk. God isn't as concerned with what we say we believe as with how we live what we believe.

If we evaluate each of these actions that help build our spiritual life, we will notice that nothing listed here is negative. And when the people, including our children, around us notice our actions, they learned how to build a relationship with God.

Another important trait that can be learned from these actions is that nothing promotes selfishness. So many times we find something that we consider special, no matter what it is, and we don't want to share. We choose to keep it only for our own self-gratification. How are we suppose to develop a true loving relationship with our Lord, if our Lord wants us to share His glory with others, and we refuse.

To add a personal note, when I was at the hospital being checked in, so that they could operate, I noticed a sheet of paper taped to the wall. As I waited for the receptionist to return, I read the paper. Once reading this paper, I felt so dumb. See, I had been trying to figure out how I should change some of my actions and how I handle myself in the flesh world. As soon as I read this small poem, it was so simple. The poem listed on the wall didn't have an author listed, but I'm sure that he or she would want it listed for all to see. When you read this poem, don't be taken in by the simplicity of it, but think about how you could use it in your daily walk with God.

"Watch Your Thoughts, They Become Words,
Watch Your Words, They Become Action,
Watch Your Action, They Become Habits,
Watch Your Habits, They Become Character,
Watch Your Character, It Becomes Your Destiny."

Now that you have read this poem, doesn't it just make since. How simple is this idea, yet so hard to achieve. For some of us, we have to deal with the politics of the fleshy world. Trying to not get taking advantage of, and try to survive. Yet, if we truly trusted in God, we wouldn't have to worry about what others thought about us. Our actions and how we handle ourselves would promote God here on Earth, and we could then allow God to take care of us, like he has already promised to do.

God calls to us today to pursue Him and to walk in His ways, to realize His purpose, and blessing. So mentor to the next generation, to your family and friends, to know and trust God. Teach them of His marvelous works so that they might grow to serve and follow Him faithfully.

Stand tall, firmly planted in God's word and love, embracing that love that you share with Him, and allowing that love to shine through all that you do. If we can live this lifestyle in all that we do, we can act as a catalyst, which will ignite the flow of our Father's love, and help transform people on a daily basis.

Your God, your Lord, in whom you trust, will make you so strong in the Lord and in the power of His might that no evil thing will befall you. As he stood with Daniel, he will make the lion's mouth close. He will shut up all that is against you; He will walk in the flame with you and keep you safe, and the favor of heaven, the smile of the most high, the kiss of His love, will make you know you are covered with the Dove.

God has a specific plan, a purpose for each and every one of us. This is designed in His infinite plan, His perfect plan. We are each given an assignment, yet he will not make us do it. We have to choose to do it. We are each here for a purpose. Our purpose might be to witness to another, and bring them to Jesus Christ. We might have a purpose to rear our children up for a special assignment. We might be here to lead entire congregations. But we can't get anywhere in the Lord's great plan if we close ourselves off from His guidance, and His wisdom.

When you accepted Jesus Christ as your Lord, and savior, you joined God's Army. By your own acceptance of Jesus Christ, you voluntarily joined God's army. And the Lord's army is a working army. Sent out on a great mission, to spread God's word. To recruit more soldiers to help spread the word. To go out, and bring more people to the safety and security of God's love. I know that we have already talked about this before, yet it is so powerful that addressing it again wouldn't hurt. But in the Book of Matthew 10:32-33, it states,

"Therefore whoever confesses Me before men, him I will also confess before my Father who is in heaven. But whoever denies Me before men, him I will also deny before my Father who is in heaven."

Now you have to admit that this scripture is pretty strong. Think of it in my profession. Being in a court of law can be intimidating. And nobody knows all the rules and regulations, the old laws and the new laws. However, if we go out and preach the word, and bring more and more people to God, on the Day of Judgment,

Jesus Christ will act as our counsel before the Father. That's pretty nice. Unless you feel that you would rather attempt to defend yourself, alone?

Think about what it cost God to love this world. Man had utterly failed in the purposes of God. All we, like sheep, have gone astray, doing our own thing, thinking, we have a clue how to live our life properly. Rather than submitting to God, we rebelled against Him. Rather than know God, we chose to ignore Him. Rather than fellowship with God, we decided to alienate ourselves from Him.

In the Book of Isaiah 53:5, it states,

"But He was wounded for our transgressions, He was bruised for our iniquities; The chastisement for our peace was upon Him, and by His stripes we are healed."

He was wounded for our transgressions, bruised for our iniquities. This literally means that Jesus was wounded for our wickedness, and bruised for our rebellion toward God. The stripes that marred Jesus' body, the pain, suffering, and humiliation that Jesus had to go through, paid the price for every sin, and every disease known to man. Jesus bore these things for us, that we might have eternal life in Heaven.

When we enrolled in God's Army we agreed to get the job done. It's our job to bring them in. Bring in the lost souls. How many people do you know? How many can you reach? You'll never know until you try. The United States Army slogan is "Uncle Sam Wants You." In God's Army we can stand on, "The price has been paid, only believe, and love God."

Do you know that Jesus grieves? Yes, He grieves. He grieves for every person that has ever died on Earth that never knew Him, and never had a chance to get to know Him. He grieves about every disease that has not been healed yet, because people don't know to bring it to Him for healing. For every one of these people that missed out on a chance to love God, that was some pain and suffering that Jesus Christ had to endure for no reason.

Do you want Jesus to quit grieving? He can, if we get the message out there. He can if we will get out there and start spreading the word. Now is the time to start, you could be a catalyst, igniting the fire of Jesus Christ, so that His glory will spread across the world, and reach all people, no matter their color, race, sex, ethnic background, and no matter where they live. And it can start today. It can start with you.

We need to start looking for opportunities to preach the gospels, tell about Jesus, and spread God's word. Opportunities arise every day, but sometimes we don't notice them, or we fail to take advantage of them.

Spreading the word of God is like building your own case for your admittance into the Kingdom of heaven. When you were saved, and gave your heart, mind, and soul to God, your name was written in the Lamb's Book of Life. Every time you do something, whether good or bad, Jesus writes it down in the Lamb's Book of Life. What will He write down beside your name? The next time you have an opportunity to witness to someone, or even help someone, think about the Lamb's Book of Life. Do you want some positive notes in there beside your name? I'm trying to get Jesus to have writer's cramp.

When you think about whether to witness or not to others about God, think of it this way. God has already asked you to spread the word. Will you tell Him no? We are all called to preach. We are all called upon by God to preach. When you think to yourself about that, I will clarify. We are all called to preach, but we are not all called to have a pulpit in a church, or on television. Where my pastor, Pastor Barbara Cannon, has been called to preach from the pulpit of the church, my wife might have been called to preach from the pulpit of her patrol vehicle, and as her position as supervisor in her shift. Our pulpit consists of where ever we are in our daily walk with God.

Jesus said, "If anyone will come after me let him deny himself, take up his cross daily and follow me. For whoever desires to save his life will lose it, but whoever loses his life for My sake will save it. (Supported by Luke 9:23-24) By this scripture alone, we can interpret that we are to put away all our personal self-serving vices, and pursue Him. We are to live like Him. If Jesus was physically here today, do you think he would be hanging out, and thinking about only himself, or do you think he would be preaching and spreading the word of God. We need to be spreading the word through our words, through our actions, and how we handle ourselves on a daily basis. The Lord multiplies those who are willing to follow Christ in all aspects of life, even if it means personal sacrifice.

You have to give both quality and a quantity of your time to train the people that you are witnessing to. You can start by telling them the wonderful and powerful stories of God's acts.

When you hit your knees in the prayer closet, pray for the people that you are witnessing to. Ask for the strength in your testimony and ask God to help you make the connection. He is there, waiting for an open invitation.

While in the middle of witnessing to another, if they seem open to your testimony, ask that you could pray with them. Lead them into that place of meekness where they can find the Lord.

Remember that while you are witnessing that you need to keep your faith strong. Know that you are on the right path and that God is listening, and watching. Don't hesitate to ask for help from Him and have courage to believe that your efforts are not in vain and falling on deaf ears.

If you have one of those persons where you get a lot of questions, or you just don't think that you can handle the situation by yourself. Ask for help from others. The pastor at your church, the elders at your church, or even a believer in the Lord are all qualified to assist you in your endeavors. That's what the church and your brothers and sisters in Christ are there for. Never give up. These people are here to assist you, since we are all working toward the same goal.

When I get someone to come to our church the first time, when they leave, I have no control over what they think, or how much they liked or disliked the service. But, I have a system that assists me in new people coming to God. My pastor and all the other people at the church now have come to know the new person, and can all act on helping this new person find Jesus.

You see, you are not alone in your quest. No one has asked you to go out and spread the word by yourself. You are only alone if that's the way you want it. But even then, the Lord is with you. All churches have a support system in place, whether advertised or not. A support system that will help its members with whatever the needs are. I use this support system to reach new potential members of the family of Christ, as well as, for personal means.

Another way that I have found resourceful is that I get a copy of the praise and worship recordings. They are usually on two different compact discs. I give them out to people who have expressed an interest in the church. After a few days, I then return to them to see what they thought of it. This usually opens up communication so that I can shed further insight that I might have that they don't. After this opportunity to witness, I still invite them in.

Sometimes new people will come to the church, and don't really like it, because of how alive it is. It is not what they are use to, or how they were brought up, or not like it is on television. Well, don't let that discourage you. Remember that we are only spreading the word of God here. They are not restricted to only go to the church that you go to. Just get them to go to a church. As long as they are active in their desires to seek God, it shouldn't matter which church that they go to.

And once they are in church regularly, then if that church is not right for them, or that church is not as alive as they need it to be as they mature and prosper, then God will assist them in changing to the right church for them. The point is that they are actively seeking the Lord now, and they weren't before. Therefore, it is a successful testimony.

You can't change the world by yourself, or over night. Take one step at a time, and witness to the people around you. Concentrate on them, and then when they take off to witness, the fire will ignite and God's word will spread like wildfire. Take one step at a time, and be diligent in your efforts. And always remember to use your support system, as well as, pray to the Father for assistance. I think that you will find that you have more than enough help to deal with your testimony.

Chapter Seven

Conclusion

Wow! We are at the conclusion already. My first publication, and it is over. Or is it? Now the journey rests on your shoulders. While reading this book, I hope and pray that you were able to gain some insight that has kept you away from that wonderful relationship with God that you desire, and that he desires. But, now the journey is yours to complete. If you shut this book, and change nothing, then nothing will change for you. So don't be like so many others, and put this book down and go on about you business like everything is great in your physical and spiritual life. Everyone needs some improvement.

As you reflect on what we have talked about, remember that it all sounds easy to complete. However, when dealing in the flesh world, we have to battle all outside inferences. You should have a little firmer grasp on how to recognize and deal with some of the thoughts in your mind that start from a negative emotion, and that dwell inside of you, making you more and more unhappy. Take a firm stance on these problem areas. Deal with them swiftly as they come up from time to time, and deal with them until they are history, and not part of you nature instincts.

Dealing with other people in the flesh world is difficult sometimes. When you experience these problems with other people, remember that they suffer just like you and I, with attacks from these negative emotions, that turn us into more and more complete sinners. Get rid of the bitterness, rage, and anger. They only end up hurting you in the end. They attack you to where your inner self is in so much pain that you outwardly turn to sin. When getting into confrontations, stay away, as best as possible, from the use of harsh words, and slanderous activity. These are only reactions that usually are defense mechanisms, in an effort to protect you from attack.

Turn these situations into opportunities to witness to others. Step out of your inner sanctum, and take a chance. I know that the first step is hard. Opening yourself up giving someone the opportunity to step on you and your feelings. But, in the end of it all, isn't the only thing important is that relationship you have with God. If your witnessing attempts, in an effort to solve this problem, bear no fruit, the Lord will still see that you are trying to accomplish what He wants us to. If you fail in your attempts, when you pray to the Father, add them in your prayers. More that likely, the first couple of steps won't work to solve problems immediately, improvement can be found later.

As you deal within yourself, think about how you are being attacked. Are they coming from some form of the seven deadly sins? Maybe there is a combination of the sins that are attacking you through your mind. Remember that these attacks are real, and they are trying to get you to turn away from God.

These seven deadly sins are gluttony, lust, greed, sloth, envy, wrath, and pride. These areas of sin are in everyday life. Make no bones about it, you will see them in some form every day. Learn to recognize them when they crop up, whether in your emotions, or that of another. Deal with them. Beat them. Not just in your self, but also in those that you come in contact with. Help others, as you would want for yourself. Jesus Christ would do it if He were here in the flesh. And since our goal on this earth is to be more and more Christ-like, we should take those steps necessary when they present themselves.

These negative emotions are attacking you through your mind to get into your heart. And your heart is where the Lord lives. Don't give up that territory. If these attacks accomplish their mission, they will eventually get your soul. Stand your ground firmly. When you recognize these attacks, and identify where they are coming from, this will give you a greater advantage to deal with them. This advantage will allow you to overcome your physical flesh, and move toward a more spiritual relationship with the Father. Conquering your flesh (taking control of it), will allow you to have more control over your emotions, thus letting you dwell in the positive emotions such as, love, joy, and peace. All of which, come from the Lord, and is where you can fellowship with Him continuously.

You can now see and evaluate how these emotions, both positive and negative, affect you lifestyle. In your daily walk with God, put away all grudges that you have. Forgive those who have offended you. Then don't be scared to ask forgiveness from those that you think you may have offended. If these people forgive you, or state that there is nothing to forgive, an opportunity to witness is upon you. Take the steps necessary to create this opportunity. Take advantage of the situation, and let others know how the Lord is working in your life. And let them know how the Lord can help them as well.

If the people you talk to will not forgive you of your offenses from the past, apologize anyway. Then later when you are in your prayer closet, pray to the Lord to touch them, and help them forgive you. Sometimes it is breath taking to see the Lord work in people, even when they don't realize it.

While you are experiencing different activities in the flesh world, stay away from the hidden dangers of participating in drinking and drug use. Both of these will swiftly lead you down the wrong road. They have mind-altering affects that will damage the progress you have made in your journey to walk with the Lord.

These vices are quite apparent everywhere. These are not hidden anywhere. They are in advertisements on television, newspapers, and the locations can be seen while you are driving to church, or the local supermarket. Besides the drinking, and drugs, also stay away from gambling and the use of profane language. These will only lead you down the wrong road as well. Gambling has been accepted widely in society today, through the use of the Internet. Even though gambling has been accepted by society, it is still wrong. Taking from another, or even putting yourself in this danger is just stupid.

Then there is the sex category. Sex is a gift from God. A gift, from God, that should be used wisely. Honor the marriage bed fully, and don't take advantage of people who are willing to violate the gift that God has given us. In addition to being against God's word, participating in sexual misconduct opens you up for all kinds of medical problems. With sexual immorality being on the rise, the spread of sexually transmitted diseases rise as well. Now some of these diseases can be cured, but not all. Is that really a chance that you are willing to take, even with the protection of some man-made device that isn't 100% effective?

Speaking in the sexual realm, what about our children? Do they see how sex has changed some of the culture of our society today? You bet they do. In my line of work, I see it all the time. I have encountered children having unprotected sexual relations at thirteen and fourteen years of age. Now, I'm not talking about a crime committed against them, but an act that they have chosen to participate in willingly. Where do you think they got the idea? Could it be television, or newspapers, or even watching us as parents act like this?

All these vices end up damaging the Temple of the Holy Spirit. That temple that the Lord has given to us to house the Holy Spirit, so that He can help us in our prayers, and assist us in reading and understanding God's word. Such a gift as this shouldn't be taken advantage of, especially when you can use it for so much good.

Our bodies are only good for so long. Back when God made the world, our bodies could last hundreds of years. But, with the addition of sin, years and years have been taken off life expectancy. Now I am talking about just the sin that surrounds us. If we choose to participate in adding additional sin to ourselves, we can expect our physical life expectancy to go down as well.

In addition to these vices, there are still some things that we do that seem to us that are really not that bad. What about smoking, and the effects of the use of tobaccos? If these other areas affect your body and damage it, wouldn't smoking, dipping, and chewing tobacco damage it as well? These are vices that seem to not bother to many people. Now I know that society has pushed us not to be allowed to use tobacco products in restaurants, and other public places. I also know that tobacco companies have been forced to advertise the physical damages that their product can cause. But has this really help us in society out? Tobacco is still used by a great majority of the population. And these efforts by society have not stopped the use, only structures where it can be used. Still though, these are vices, vices that damage our bodies, and cause our life expectancy to go down. If you participate in these, you are only doing yourself an injustice. You are not allowing yourself a chance to walk completely free with the Lord. Stop these vices now; gain control of your life. Life is precious; God gave it to us to fellowship with Him. We can't if we have these vices holding us back, or are not here to fellowship with Him.

All of this damages the Temple of the Holy Spirit. By damaging the temple where the Holy Spirit dwells, we take the chance of offending the Holy Spirit. Now if the Holy Spirit is our connection to the Father, offending Him doesn't help us one bit. If we have offended the Holy Spirit, we have to mend that area of our life, and build that relationship again, so that we can continue our journey with the Lord.

So stay aware of these problem areas, and make any adjustments that you need to in an effort to make progress, instead of regressing. When you think that you have these problems handled, then you will be catapulted forward in your relationship with God.

With this new rationale of thinking, you can start you spiritual quest to fellowship with God completely. You will have the opportunity to start walking closer and closer with God on a daily basis. Apply the "Fruits of the Holy Spirit" in your daily regiment. By adding these positive elements, you can only gain further and further in your spiritual walk with God.

Adding these fruits such as, love, joy, peace, long-suffering, kindness, goodness, faithfulness, gentleness, and self-control will make tremendous changes in your persona. Changes that will be apparent to all others that have known your and how you were before. With people that you meet new, the lifestyle that you lead through these fruits, will also be quite apparent, and noticeable. So noticeable, people will wonder what is going on with you, and why is there such a change. These are good reactions, because most people in our society are curious. And as their curiosity grows they will ask you of these changes. Even though at this stage you are still working on yourself, when they come and ask you about these changes, there arises an opportunity to witness, and bring more fruit to God. And all you had to do was earnestly want to change for the better in yourself. Through these changes in your own being, you will have the opportunity to lead someone else to Jesus Christ.

Each day take with you some of the fruits. Make an effort to use them more and more in your daily walk. As your invest time and effort in to using more of these positive emotions, you will find that you are witnessing and affecting others by the way you walk, talk, and handle yourself. This kind of witnessing takes little outward work on your part. See, by improving within yourself, you still cause others to take notice of the greatly improved lifestyle that you have. When they take notice, it causes a positive change in them to want to be that happy, and cheerful as you.

Changing of these positive emotions will also bring notice from the Father. As these changes take place, the more ability you will have to utilize the "Gifts of the Holy Spirit" that the Father wants to give to you. In time, God will see the tremendous improvements that you have made in your life, and how now you are becoming more Christ-Like. When God thinks that the time is right, the gift or gifts that He bestowed upon you will be tremendous. Take these gifts to heart, and treat them with the respect that they deserve. Use them properly, and not for your own personal gratification. Praise God more and more with these gifts, and edify the church properly.

Mostly we have talked about the changing of our lifestyle in the public eye. When I say public, I also mean in front of our family, friends, church members, and anyone that can see us in action. These changes are good, and must have resulted in some fruit bearing by now, even if we haven't noticed it. But changing our lifestyle is only part of the equation. We still have things that we need to do both in private and in public to do our part for God.

Let's start with reading the Bible. Now, I'm not going to say I am the greatest at this, but I like to read the Bible mostly at night. I tend to turn off the television set, after the children have gone to bed, and just read the Bible. I also like to read the Bible aloud. I don't know that it has any better or worst effect for me, but I seem to enjoy it more aloud. I like to read the Bible, and after a couple of passages, study the meaning of the scriptures. I try to place the message in my life. I like to see if the message is something I could have used already in my life, and how with this new found knowledge, would have potentially changes the outcome.

Sometimes when I read the Bible, it still doesn't click in my mind. I study the passage, look over the notes, and check out the references. Then when it still doesn't come together for me, I have to go to the Internet and check for some commentaries from Bible scholars to get the answers that I need. And if that doesn't work for me, I then have to make notes and talk to my pastor about it. When I check with my pastor, she provides some insight into what I am missing. These are all steps that I take to understand God's mighty word. Sometimes it takes longer to understand than I would like it to, but time is a little price compared to understanding what God has intended for us.

I suggest that when you start your journey through the Bible, that you take the additional steps necessary to come to a complete understanding of the Bible. Rushing through the Bible, just to say that you have read the whole thing serves no purpose. Understanding God's word serves a better purpose.

When I read, I like to pray before hand, and ask for God's word to be opened up for me to understand. I know upfront that I am not educationally experienced enough to understand it on my own. Once I am finished praying, I then sit down to read, study, and devour the Bible. Once completed for that session, I close my studies up with another prayer. I pray thankfulness for what God has given us and for what I might have learned that night.

I suggest that you do the same thing. Pray before reading the Bible. Pray for understanding, it can't hurt. Then close with prayer thanking Him for all that He means to you. I think that you will find the experience fulfilling.

I also like to take the Bible with me to work. Sometimes when the pressures of the day start to creep up on me, or an opportunity to witness comes available, the Bible is a great resource to have close by. Just like when an umpire or referee take the field, if they had the rule book with them, and were not afraid to use it, they would get most of the calls right to start with.

While you are on your journey seeking the Lord, don't take the trip alone. Sometimes, we need a little alone time to refresh ourselves, and our temperament, however, on this quest for knowledge, take your family with you. Train your children on the stories of God's great accomplishments. Teach them how to read the Bible. The pay off in the long run, is that they will always have a close relationship with God, and will be able to lead one day with the help of the Lord, rather than being without the Lord, and knowing and trusting in Him.

The children are the future. They are the ones that will lead this nation, this world one day. Give them now the educational structure that they need to survive when these challenges come before them.

During your quest, plan on fasting from time to time, offering up a truly blessed sacrifice to the Lord. When fasting comes around, work in more study time on God's word, and pray more diligently. The more sincere you are to the Lord during these times, the greater payoff you will achieve. Remember that every time you fast and give this kind of sacrifice to the Lord, it becomes a memorial to Him, presented to Him in the throne room, in the Kingdom of Heaven.

The next thing to address is prayer. When should you pray? Well I think the answer is rather simple for me. I like to pray when I get up in the morning, pray before my meals, pray before I go to bed, pray before I go to work, and then pray anytime the thought of prayer enters my mind. Now I am not saying that all of these prayers are lengthy. Some of these prayers are short and sweet and straight to the point.

Praying though is an act of fellowship with the Father. Man was created in the beginning for fellowship with God, and I am going to fellowship with Him. Now there is more than one kind of prayer. Most of the time, I am just thanking Him for all that He has done for me. I don't think that I can thank Him enough for this, that He has allowed me to have. Especially with the way I started off my life, living in sin, and wasting a lot of valuable time that could have been spent with Him.

In addition to the thankful prayers, there are the need prayers. These prayers are generated in an effort to gain something with the Lord assistance. Whether giving over the burdens that we carry to Him, or requesting some insight into the Bible. The need prayers encompass a great deal, which would be too lengthy to cover in this area. But prayer is necessary. Prayer is important.

Prayer is very important in that we are allowed to thank God for it all, ask of Him what we will, and receive from Him the changing and transforming that is necessary to become more Christ-Like in our walk with God.

And lastly, witnessing. Witnessing is very important. If we are to become more Christ-Like in our efforts on earth, witnessing is a tremendous portion of what we need to do. When the opportunity comes up we have to step forward and give our testimony, tell of the glorious stories and accomplishments of the Lord, and invite others in to such a wonderful place of fellowship with the Father.

Without witnessing, others will be lost forever in the pit of Hell for eternity. And as we have discussed before, it grieves Jesus Christ when some pass without the opportunity to grow and know His love.

Notes from outside the realm of this book

If you haven't noticed, there is a revival going on. A revival going on that is bringing more and more of your brothers and sisters in Christ back to the fold. This revival that I am talking about is going on everywhere. That's what I got caught up in. A revival where we, as a Christian nation, are striving forward walking the walk, and talking the talk of our Lord Jesus Christ. We are out there everyday trying to spread the word, and sing God's praises. Now is the time to take the steps necessary to gain in your strength the power of the Lord. Now is the time to grow in your relationship with the Lord.

We are all called to preach. Some are called to preach on television. Some are called to preach in the pulpit of a church. Some are called to preach in their patrol car. Some are called to preach from their office. Some are called to spread the word from their position as a waitress, or a baggage handler. Some are called to spread God's word through music, dance, or some other talent that has been instilled in you. But the point is, WE HAVE ALL BEEN CALLED!

The time is now to get busy. When you are out there giving your testimony, and preaching God's word, you will be asked, "Are You Wholly?" Well are you? The answer is, "YES!"Once you accepted the Lord Jesus Christ into your heart and were truly saved, you became wholly. The Lord is within you. If Christ has taken over you inside, doesn't He make you wholly? Yes, He does! All you have to do is tap into what He has given you.

God's message right now is, "Close the Lion's Mouth." The lion is the devil. Stand up and be strong. Close that lion's mouth today. We are mortal. But we can win. Jesus Christ was mortal when He was on earth. Daniel was mortal, Stephen was mortal, and all the great brothers and sisters in the Bible were mortal. They all closed the lion's mouth. Now is you time. Let's work together and close that lion's mouth now and forever!

I thank you for reading this book, and I pray that you have gained something positive from it. When you are finished reading this book, share it with another. Give this book to another, or purchase another as a gift for someone. Spread the word about the glorious love of our Father.

I leave you as my brothers and sisters in Christ, thankful the Lord has allowed me to accomplish this experience. I have learned so much through these efforts, and challenge each and every one of you to witness and testify to what you know and have learned. With all my love, thank you, and I'll see you one day in the Kingdom of Heaven, if not before then.

Appendix

Posted Sermons

During my injury time my Pastor, Pastor Barbara Cannon, asked me to preach during our weekly Wednesday Night meetings. The follow pages contain some of the ten minutes sermons that I presented at His Freedom Reigns Ministries. I provide these with an open heart to each and every one of you who will read them. Follow along with the meanings in these sermons, and apply them to your own life.

I also will tell you that researching and preparing a sermon, presenting it to a group of people that you know well, can be quite intimidating. It is hard work, but the sensation of happiness and joy that you receive after can't be described in words. If you get the chance to witness to your congregation, or share some research that has interested you, I challenge you to ask for that time at church to present your information, and follow through on your mission to accomplish this. The rewards far outweigh the stress that will be placed upon you. Besides, is there a better way to show God that you are thinking about Him, and worshipping Him than in your very own church?

Anyway, here are the sermons that I talked about, Please enjoy!

Hindrances of the Gifts

Tonight's message is self-serving. I have found some answers to questions that I have been researching, and I am going to pass them along to you. This will give me peace of mind to know that I may have helped someone, plus it has added benefit that I will not forget what I have learned.

Pastor Barbara has started to take us toward our journey seeking spiritual gifts. Brother Donnie has warned us of the effects of lying, and how lying will separate us from the will of God. Since God is not capable of lying, this act on our behalf will tear the bond that we have with God.

Now I am here to ensure that we know how to stay on the path to receiving these gifts, and not to get side tracked in some areas. I do not know all the answers, and don't claim to, but I have a few points that I need to make to ensure that we stay on the path.

In Matthew 6:33, and Jesus said,

"But seek first the kingdom of God and His righteousness, and all these things shall be added to you."

This scripture shows that we should not be preoccupied with material things of this earth; our attention should be to seek God's kingdom and righteousness. And we should know that as we do this, God will add all these things to us. This is a covenant of faithfulness that the Lord will respond, as long as we seek Him. But we have to get right in ourselves first before the Lord will provide. We have to be earnest and sincere.

I questioned for a while, why I haven't received an answer to my prayers, and received these gifts. Of course,

I was waiting for the gifts. That was supposed to be the answer to these prayers.

Then while doing some research in another book, I found the answer. I have received the answer to my prayers. As we start our journey seeking the Lord, we sometimes forget that the Lord acts as our Father. Now how many times have our parents given us everything that we have wanted? It just doesn't happen all the time. Well, the same thing occurs with God. God can see in our hearts and in our minds, and knows more about us than we know. God finds out if we are ready for the gifts and whether we can handle these gifts. He finds out if we can utilize these gifts to glorify his name, and edify the church, or would we be subject to use them for personal motives.

Fortunately, God sometimes answers prayers with a No! Sometimes, the answer is not yet. But these are answers. So in a sense we do get our prayers answered, we just sometimes don't like the answers.

We should put God's kingdom first in our lives. This is the first step on the pathway to where we can learn to determine His will, purpose, and call on our life.

We should first turn toward His word. This is the pathway to understanding His will for us. As we do this, we should learn to recognize His way as we hear the voice of His Spirit as it directs us.

Then we have to pay attention to the small, still, little voice that we can all hear. God's will, won't come in a lightning bolt from the sky, or a great ball of fire, but will be apparent to us in small events and things that can ultimately determine our destiny with the Lord. But, we have to pay attention. If we are so busy with the things of the flesh world, we will lose contact with the steps that the Lord has placed for us to help guide us into the path of righteousness that he has laid before us.

I once had a question. The question was simply, how do I know God is talking to me, and it isn't the devil, or my own personal self, seeking gratification. That small voice, that is in your head? Do you know what I'm talking about? How do we know that it is the voice of the Lord? How do we know it is not the voice of the devil, or some demonic force? Are we being misled by voices?

In 1 John 4:1, it states,

"Beloved, do not believe every spirit, but test the spirits, whether they are of God; because many false prophets have gone out into the world."

Well, the scripture tell us to test the voice. That is one of the few times where we are allowed testing. When you hear the voice, challenge the voice with, "Did Jesus come in the flesh?" The devil and his demonic forces will not acknowledge such a feat, and the Holy Spirit knows it is the truth and will let you know it.

These spirits know who we are, and what we are about. They can tell where we stand in our relationship with the Lord. This increases our vulnerability to attacks. I can't confess that I have ever been through this, but from what I have read, I realize that we have to pay close attention to what these spirits say. Remember as I have stated before, it is those little things that can determine whether we stay on the path or not.

In Matthew 8:29, in speaking of two men who were possessed by demons, who were causing quite a stir among the community there, and they saw Jesus as he approached. The Bible states that they said,

"And suddenly they cried out, saying, What have we to do with you, Jesus, you son of God? Have you come here to torment us before the time?"

134

Now let's look at this passage closely. These two demons were causing quite a bit of problems in the community, yet when they recognized Jesus, the Son of God, they questioned whether He had come to torment them. Well, how quickly they forget about the torment and suffering that they caused. Sounds a lot like Jacob, when he became mad at Laden for deceiving him, even though he was a deceiver to his own father. But, back to these demons, I interpret this scripture in such a way that it actually sounds like the demons are fearful of Jesus, and rightly so, they should be. But these demons are fearful; because they think what they are doing is all right. They think they have the right to cause pain and torment, because it is not time for their end. By the scriptures, it states that they asked if Jesus came to torment them before the time. Before the time. Well, it doesn't take a brain surgeon to figure out that they know Jesus is the one, he's the man! Jesus is capable of destroying them, and that they are going to be destroyed. Their big question was, is it time already. They wanted to know if it is the Day of Judgment.

So these demons, or spirits knew who Jesus was. They also know who we are, and where we stand in our relationship with God.

When we hear that voice in our head, we need to "test the spirits." When the devil came to test Jesus, and I am not going to go into a lot of detail about this, but when Jesus was tested by the devil, every time the devil said something to Him it started with "If."

1) IF you are the Son of God, command that these stones become bread.
2) IF you are the Son of God, throw yourself down.
3) All these things I will give you, IF you will fall down and worship me.

It seems that everything that comes from the devil and his demonic force is contingent on you doing something for him, and then he will provide whatever the bribe is. When the devil or demonic force comes after us, what are they using to attack us with? They are using the seven deadly sins to attack us through. Think about it?

These seven deadly sins are man-made, and work to provide us materialistic things of the flesh that we really don't need. Lust, Greed, Sloth, Wrath, Envy, Pride, and Gluttony. These seven deadly sins are the doorway for the devil to take control of our soul. They attack us through the flesh worlds passions and desires that bring some sort of respectability in this world, at least, respectability in our own minds.

The devil makes false promises and false statements that attack us and pull us away from the inner circle of faith that we have in Jesus Christ. So, and according to the scriptures, we must test these spirits; test the voices that you hear. If they won't confess that Jesus came in the flesh, then they are wrong, and are not of God. Forget about them, and do away with them. Fall down on your knees and pray for assistance, pray for strength to battle this problem. Let the Lord know that the devil or some demonic force is trespassing upon his territory, and ask that He deal with them swiftly and permanently.

So, what keeps us away from the spiritual gifts that we so desire? We have to improve in ourselves. In an effort to get these spiritual gifts, we have to achieve the fruits of the spirit.

In Galatians 5:22-23, it states,

"But the fruit of the spirit is love, joy, peace, long-suffering, kindness, goodness, faithfulness, gentleness, self-control. Against such there is no law."

The first three, love, joy, and peace, concern our own personal attitude. The second three, longsuffering, kindness, goodness, deals with social relationships, and the third three, faithfulness, gentleness, self-control, deal with our conduct as Christians.

If you will think about these fruits of the Holy Spirit, you will notice that none of them are self-serving. There are no fruits that fall in line with the passions and desires of the seven deadly sins. To put it another way, the fruits of the Holy Spirit do not serve the passions and desires of this world. They lead us to something better. They lead us to the Kingdom of God, a place far better than anything this world has to offer.

So when you hit your knees and pray to the Lord, when we ask Him for the spiritual gifts that we all want so badly, remember to first ask for the fruits of the Holy Spirit. Just like when we eat dinner with our family, our Father doesn't want us to have dessert before we have the main course.

The end of this sermon.

The Gift (Christmas)

I hope everyone had a wonderful Christmas. I had a great Christmas. As some of you know, Jennifer and I are both police officers, and sometimes we have to work on Christmas Day. Plus you add the pressures of having children from previous relationships, and it can make a mockery out of planning Christmas events with our children, and our extended families. However, because of this injury that I sustained, I was able to accommodate all plans and that made this a very nice Christmas for me where I was able to see and visit all my family.

Now because of work and timing, we were able to spend some Christmas time at home with our children, visit my parents, visit Jennifer's parents, and coordinate to basically see everyone in our family without anyone else having to give or take in the planning stages of Christmas time. This was the first time every in my life that there was no fussing about when I could have the kids, what time I had to have them somewhere, and so on. This Christmas was absolutely the most stress free Christmas that I have ever had.

Now with all the hustle and busell of the Christmas season, the activities and the traveling around, one can lose track of what is important, and what this season is all about. Between purchasing all the gifts that we need to have, making all the arrangements to see everyone, cooking all the foods that are necessary to supply such great feast for family and friends, we sometimes forget what is important.

When talking about Christmas gifts that we have purchased, one of the most important aspects of the Christmas present itself is the tag. Can you imagine during the passing out of presents, one could come without a tag? And now the massive investigation ensues to find its origin, in an effort, to find where it needs to go.

So what are tags? Tags generally come in different colors, and sometimes have different images on them, but most all have the same thing...To: and From:

Most of us know what kind of gift we are getting, once we know who it is from. That's why the from category is so important. Certain people in your life know you so well that they always give you something that you need, or will need and use in the near future.

Most people who give me gifts love me to some degree or another. I still have some gifts from my children from years gone by. Almost all of them said, I Love You, Dad, and they are more valuable to me than gold or silver. I can absolutely state that the police officer nutcracker, and the magnetic fish thermostat that I received this year can never be bought from me. And that is just a few of the many that I have received over the years.

When you are given a gift, you have a responsibility. Did you know that? Yes, you have a responsibility. You have to either accept the gift, or refuse the gift. Now I know that sounds pretty stupid, however, it is true. I realize this sounds simple, but in order for someone to give a gift, it must be received. If you don't accept it you will never know what it is and you will never be able to use it. God is giving us a gift. A gift that is free. God is giving us a gift that we don't have to earn or work for to achieve. If you accept this gift you will cherish and use it as part of your life.

Remember I said earlier that some people know you so well that they give us something that we need, or will use. So, do you think God is any different?

John 3:16,

"For God so loved the world, he gave his only begotten son, that whoever believe in him should not perish but have everlasting life."

For God so loved me. The God of Heaven, the creator loves me. Wow, that is awesome. He has the entire resources of heaven, so this should be the most valuable gift I could ever receive.

So what does love mean? We all have an unwritten idea of what it means, but to put it to words sometimes is hard. Love means an unselfish, loyal concern for the good of another. Which is also an unconditional good feeling for another.

Scriptures show that God showed his great love for us by sending Christ to die for us while we were still sinners, who had no relationship with him. (Romans 5:8) Do you see how tremendous that is? Think of it in the world today. Could you imagine someone, or some company offering this kind of deal to people who didn't know they existed? There is no money in that, no guarantee. It is unheard of. Yet, God did it!

When we receive his gift, we can't help but fall in love with him. It is so tremendous and so special. God should be the greatest love of our life. It states in Matthew 22:37-39, Jesus said to him (a lawyer),

"You shall love the Lord your God with all your heart, with all your soul. And with your entire mind. This the first and great commandment, And the second is like it; You shall love your neighbor as yourself."

It kind of takes your breath away. How simple are these words, yet how hard are these words to perform in our daily life.

Before we can fully love one another, we must fully love God and understand his love for us. That is pretty deep, also. Our love for others should model Christ's love for us. (Ephesians 5:1-2)

I love to watch kids open presents. They begin ripping and tearing at the paper. They are so eager to find out what's inside. They don't care about the bows, paper, or boxes. Nothing seems to matter except to get the gift and start using it. God desires that same excitement and intensity with his gift.

For God so loved you and me that he gave his one and only son. The gift God desires to give us is his son, Jesus

Christ. If we don't accept the gift we will never be able to know, or use the gift.

Once we accept the gift, he desires us to get excited about using the gift. Just like the kids, we are to find out all we can so we can fully utilize and live with the gift, the gift of Jesus. The Bible tells us, to abide in him. What does that mean? Well, I looked it up. Abide means to wait for, or to endure without yielding.

What do we have to do with God's only son, accept him. It is that simple. You can receive that gift tonight, but you must be willing to accept the gift. What are the benefits of the son? Part of learning about the Gift of Jesus is everlasting life, joy, peace, and a relationship with God that cannot be attained any other way.

That brings me to regifting. Everybody makes a big deal about regifting. It has become an acceptable practice in our culture. We use to call it hand-me-downs. The greatest thing about God's gift is that once you have accepted the gift, he wants you to go out and re-gift it to others.

A Christian who understands what love truly means and shows love in his or her life is the greatest testimony to others. The depth of our love for God directly affects our ability to minister to others. The love we have for those around us is an indication of the strength of our Christian walk. The closer we grow to God, the more our love for others should increase.

And some of you think that you can't witness to others. You don't know how. Well, every believer has a testimony. Some may be more drastic than others. But, regardless of how incredible or not your testimony may seem, your personal salvation story will help you find common ground with a non-believer. You can tell of your former life and the attitudes that you had before coming to Christ, then explain the changes that were made in your life so you could come to Christ, and how that has worked out for you. When a non-believer sees that you can relate to his or her own life, he or she may be open to what you have to say.

Remember, that the burden doesn't have to rely upon your shoulders alone, invite them to church. You have a working support system here. We as the members of this church will help you in your mission to save others.

So when we talk about the Christmas season, and you examine how your holiday season went, did you receive that greatest gift ever known to man? And more important…Did you help give it?

John 3:16;

"For God so loved the world that He gave His only begotten Son that whoever believes in Him should not perish but have everlasting life."

I will conclude this message tonight with a short story that describes this message greatly. This story came by way of the Internet, and it is from an unknown author.

A little boy was selling newspapers on the corner; the people were in and out of the cold. The little boy was so cold that he wasn't trying to sell many papers. He walked up to a policeman and said, "Mister, you wouldn't happen to know where a poor boy could find a warm place to sleep tonight, would you? You see, I sleep in a box around the corner, and down the alley and it gets awful cold in there at night. Sure would be nice to have a warm place to stay."

The policeman looked down at the little boy and said, "You go down the street to that big white house and you knock on the door. When they come out the door, you just say, John 3:16,and they will let you in."

So he did, he walked up the steps and knocked on the door, and a lady answered. He looked up and said, John 3:16, and the lady said come on in, son.

She took him in and she sat him down in a split bottom rocker in front of a great big old fireplace, and she went off. The boy sat there for a while and thought to himself, John 3:16, I don't understand it, but it sure makes a cold boy warm.

Later she came back and asked him, Are you hungry, and he said, well just a little, I haven't eaten in a couple of days, and I guess I could stand a little bit of food.

The lady took him in the kitchen and sat him down to a table full of wonderful food. He ate and ate until he couldn't eat anymore. Then he thought to himself, John 3:16, boy I sure don't understand it, but it sure makes a hungry boy full.

She took him upstairs to a bathroom to a huge bathtub filled with warm water and he sat there and soaked for a while. As he soaked, he thought to himself, John 3:16...I don't understand it, but it sure makes a dirty boy clean. You know, I've not had a bath, a real bath in my whole life. The only bath I ever had was when I stood in front of that big old fire hydrant as they flushed it out.

The lady came in and got him. She took him to a room, tucked him into a big old feather bed, pulled the covers up around his neck, kissed him goodnight and turned out the lights. As he laid in the darkness and looked out the window at the snow coming down on that cold night, he thought to himself, John 3:16...I don't understand it, but it sure makes a tired boy rested.

The next morning the lady came back up and took him down again to the same big table full of food. After he ate, she took him back to that same big old split bottom rocker in front of the fireplace and picked up a big old Bible.

She sat down in front of him and looked into his young face. Do you understand John 3:16? She asked gently. He replied, no ma'am, I don't. The first time I ever heard it was last night when the policeman told me to use it.

She opened the Bible to John 3:16 and began to explain to him about Jesus. Right there in front of that big old fireplace, he gave his heart and life to Jesus. He sat there and thought John 3:16...I don't understand it, but it sure makes a lost boy feel safe.

You know, I have to confess I don't understand it either. How God was willing to send his son to die for me. And how Jesus would agree to do such a thing. I don't understand the agony of the father and every angel in heaven as they watched Jesus suffer and die. I don't understand the intense love for me that kept Jesus on the cross till the end. I don't understand it, but it sure does make life worth living.

John 3:16,

"For God so loved the world, that he gave his only begotten Son that whosoever believeth in Him should not perish but have everlasting life."

The end of this sermon.

New Year's Time

Now lets talk about television. What is television? Television use to be solely a form of entertainment, but now it is used for advertisements, news, talk shows, gossip, make believe fake shows that make a mockery of traditional clean family living, and there is so much more. But, have I answered the question?

What is television? Well, from what I have seen as of late, television is the most common source of evil there is in the world today. Now, I am not saying for you to go home and throw your television set out. The machine, itself, is just a machine. But what we as a society have allowed to be placed on that television set is absolutely pitiful, and it goes into every home on the planet, most all night-time establishments, and just about in every eating establishment that you could visit.

Now if our problem isn't bad enough as parents, where we attempt to raise our children in a good Christian foundation, we have to battle this nightmare. We are alone in this battle. Just you, The Lord, and me. Think about it, we can't even get assistance from public schools.

I was watching a television documentary the other day on one of those history channels, which one I don't know. The name of the show had to do with someone finding John the Baptist's home. Now the program lasted about an hour. And don't get me wrong, the program was very informative, however as so many television shows do, they provide just enough information both for and against their own subject matter to where they don't take a stance supporting or denying the story format.

What does that do to the viewing public? If the show doesn't provide all the material necessary for the viewing audience, how can we make a credible decision? Therefore, they script the show to leave some doubt. Why? Because we are a doubting society, unless proof is given. As I have said before, we are a stiff-necked group of people who always seem to need visual, and physical examples to prove something.

Now to make sense of what I am talking about. Everybody knows what a court of law is and how it relates to the proving of guilt or innocence. In our courts of today, all a defendant has to do is provide a reasonable doubt in one persons mind to be set free.

Creating doubt however, let's the networks keep there funding, and doesn't cause them any problems by them taking a stand. Remember Christmas! For most companies, and corporations, it's Season's Greetings, or Happy Holidays. What happened to Merry Christmas?

So when talking about television, are we couch potatoes? Think about your time in front of the television set. How much time is truly wasted? I know as an example that I might watch a show at 8pm, then look at the TV Guide channel to only find that the next show I want to watch comes on at 10pm. Well, what I am going to do till then? I'm going to find another show to watch, or a rerun, or something that I am not really interested in to pass the time away.

Wasted time. Just not with the television, but in other areas of your life as well. Do you have wasted time? Take a look at your schedule this week and be honest with yourself. Find out if you have wasted time. I will be honest with you. I have hours. Sometimes I lay in bed for a couple of hours till I can go to sleep.

Let's talk about how to fill these time slots up. We're talking about New Year's Resolutions here. My resolutions are:

1) Lose Weight
2) Read, Study, and Devour the Bible
3) Pray more daily
4) Bring double the people this year to the Lord
5) Seek God's Will & Live in His Power

Now how am I going to accomplish this task?

I voluntarily joined God's Army. I am a soldier of the Lord. And the Lord's Army is a working army. I don't bear rank that allows me to sit behind a desk, shout

out orders to others, and rest prideful, thinking; I am a soldier of the Lord. No, I need to get busy. And I say to you, we all need to get busy.

We are accountable in God's Army. In the New Testament it is mentioned at least seven times about accountability. In 1 Corinthians 3:8-9, it states,

"Now he who plants and he who waters are one, and each one will receive his own reward according to his labor. For we are God's fellow workers; you are God's field, you are God's building."

What does this mean? This means that you watch my back and I will watch yours. We are in God's Army together working for the same result. Working together to bring more people to the Lord. Now is the time, where we are allowed to be recruiter's. We are recruiter's for the most glorious army ever known. God's Army.

When the time comes, do you want to be standing on the battlefield in a small number, or a larger number? Don't get me wrong, due to the love of my Lord, and the faith I have in Him, I will stand on the battle line alone, if need be, but I might as well take some company with me. I would hate that my family and friends would miss out on such a blessing.

But aren't we supposed to spread the word. Isn't that our duty and our obligation, because of our commitment to the Lord?

Commitment

In Matthew 13:21, it states,

"yet he has no root in himself, but endures only for a while. For when tribulation or persecution arises because of the word, immediately he stumbles."

What does that tell you? It tells us that we as soldiers of God are accountable to the Lord for young Christians. And I would go as far as to say, we are accountable for all Christians. Going back to what I said earlier. You watch my back and I'll watch yours, and together we can succeed.

In Matthew 10:32-33, it states,

"Therefore whoever confesses Me before men, him I will confess before My Father who is in heaven. But whoever denies Me before men, him I will also deny before My Father who is in heaven."

What does that tell you? Well it says that Jesus Christ will stand up for you and I in front of God, if we stay committed. But it states, that we will be denied if we falter on our end of the bargain. Now I poise a question for you to answer to yourself, are we living up to our end of the bargain by staying within ourselves with God's Word, or should we share the beautiful, and powerful word?

While you ponder the question, I'll share with you scripture from Acts 14:21-22, where it states,

"And when they preached the gospel to that city and made many disciples, they returned to Lystra, Iconium, and Antioch strengthening the souls of the disciples, exhorting them to continue in the

faith, and saying we must through many tribulations enter the kingdom of God."

Wow, it states right there, go out and bring people to Jesus, and encourage and help keep strong those who have already joined the Army of God.

Now, I will not lie to you. It sounds easy, but there will be obstacles. And I say that there are two things in this world; one is fear, the other faith. One belongs to the devil, the other to God. If you believe in God, there is no fear. If you sway toward any delusion of Satan, you will be brought into fear. And fear always brings bondage. There is a place of perfect love fro Christ in which you are always casting out all fear and you are living in the place of freedom (1 John 4:18). Be sure that you never allow anything to make you afraid. God is for you; who can be against you? (Romans 8:3)

So, in conclusion, I challenge each and every one of you here to meet or exceed my resolution for this upcoming year. Having faith in the Lord works. By doing the Lord's work, we will be able to bear fruit. Bear fruit for the Lord.

And lastly, you are not alone, for the Lord will be with you.

The end of this sermon.

My Suffering Savior

I would like to thank you all for coming here tonight, as you have every other night. You had the knowledge that a novice would be in the pulpit, yet you still showed up. The support you have showed has given me purpose in this ministry. I became saved for real in this church, and now thanks to you, and Pastor Barbara, I am on fire for God. And later, when you see me as a powerful man of God, you will know that you helped create this. I thank you and I love you.

Now let's talk about love. I love each and every one of you in here tonight. And I realized earlier this week that I love every other person in this world. Good, bad, or indifferent. I realized this, because of the grief and sadness that I felt when I was given the word for tonight.

Man, in his effort to govern himself, has fouled things up so bad; it will take God to straighten things out. Before, we as human beings fouled things up, and the Lord would send Judges to correct the problems that we created. But then it got so bad, that a normal one or two people wouldn't have been able to make a dent in the problems that we had created. Now in God's Word it tells of the Messiah coming to rescue us several hundred years before he was to come. And...

In Isaiah 53:5, it states,

"But He was wounded for our transgressions, He was bruised for our iniquities; The chastisement for our peace was upon Him, and by His stripes we are healed."

He was wounded for our transgressions, bruised for our iniquities. This literally means that Jesus was wounded for our wickedness, and bruised for our rebellion toward God.

Think about what it cost God to love this world. Man had utterly failed in the purposes of God. All we, like sheep, have gone astray, doing our own thing, thinking, we have a clue how to live our life properly. Rather than submitting to God, we rebelled against God. Rather than know God, we chose to ignore Him. Rather than fellowship with God, we decided to alienate ourselves from God.

So we are partly responsible for the suffering and the death of Jesus Christ, because he suffered and died for me, that he might bring me the forgiveness of my sins. That he may bring me into fellowship with God. God created man, in the beginning, for fellowship. Fellowship was broken when man turned away from God and sinned. For us to have this fellowship again, something has to happen. And that is why Jesus came, that he might take the guilt of sin. That because of his death, I can come closer to God and love him, and have fellowship.

Now, to bring this to light for tonight's purpose. Because this happened two thousand years ago, what does this mean to us? Well, imagine each person that has died from the time Jesus Christ died that was unsaved. Imagine every person that went through his or her life not healed. Imagine every person that has ever breathed on this planet, who has never known God and his awesome power.

The stripes that marred Jesus' body, the pain, suffering, humiliation, and etc. that Jesus had to go through. That paid the price for every sin, and every disease known. Jesus bore these things for us, that we might have eternal life in Heaven. He paid the price up front. He didn't wait to see how much the price was for us, he paid a lump sum, up front, because the amount of the price didn't matter.

Now imagine, Jesus looking down on this world, and every time he sees a disease not healed, every time he sees a lost soul die, not saved. He grieves. He grieves for that lost soul, or that person in anguish, because he made the payment, he didn't miss a payment, he wasn't late on any payments because he didn't tote the note. He paid up front, full price. And so he grieves… and we should to, to some extent.

When we enrolled in God's Army, we agreed to get the job done. It's our job to bring them in. Bring in the lost souls. When looking at a recruiting poster for the United States Army, it says Uncle Sam wants you. In God's Army, we can stand on the saying the price has already been paid, only believe, and love GOD. If you need a pitch to start with try, come join me at the free buffet. My Lord offers hope for the helpless, rest for the weary, love for the broken heart, grace and forgiveness, mercy and healing, and he'll meet you wherever you are. At the Lord's buffet, take all you want.

Let's put it another way. Imagine an arcade machine sitting over here in the corner. The name of the game is, "The Game of Eternal Life." You have no joystick, and no place to put money. There is only two buttons, that state, I accept Jesus Christ, or I deny Jesus Christ. You look up at the display and see that the game has unlimited credits. When this world is over, when Jesus comes back and takes you and me to heaven, this machine is still going to have unused credits on it. It is our job to get those credits used. Any unused credits are just a little more that Jesus had to endure, for no reason. So, He grieves.

Now, how do we do it? Well, we have to stop being only listeners to God's Word. We have to start being a doer. We can't go from one meeting to another, one church then another, one special speaker to another. We have to make a commitment. We got to get out and start doing what we have learned. We have to utilize the information of life that we have gained.

We need to start looking for opportunities to preach the gospel, tell about Jesus, and spread God's Word.

Opportunities arise everyday, but sometimes we don't notice them or fail to take advantage of them.

I'll give you an example of one. The other day, I was riding home and I decided to call a friend that I had not talked to for a couple of months. My friend is a church-goer, and he works as a counselor at some church field trips occasionally. He told me that he and his wife were still trying to get pregnant, but haven't had any luck yet. Immediately, I recognized this as an opportunity. So I let him tell me about his upcoming appointment to a fertility doctor, and he asked what I thought. I told him that I knew a doctor that had some good luck in the field of helping people out who wanted to have a child. He stated that was great, and so I hit him with it, I said let me tell you the doctor's name, it will be pretty easy to remember. He said go ahead, and then I told him.

I said, don't call him doctor because he doesn't really go by that name. Well, my friend's attention perked up, and he was very inquisitive. I said, His name is Jesus Christ, and tell him I referred you. After a short pause, he came back with I'm impressed. He wasn't expecting that. So I went on to tell him about Rachel and Leah going through some barren times for Jacob, and then about Hanna being barren for so long then having a child, Samuel, who turned out to be a powerful man of God.

My friend then stated that he was going to have to go to the fertility doctor because of his wife's request, but was going to work on my suggestion immediately, and asked that I pray for them as well. Then he thanked me, and asked me out to dinner, and then the conversation was concluded.

The rest of the drive home was so peaceful. If anybody had seen me they probably would have noticed a glow about me. I had the opportunity to spread the word, and it even put me up in a better frame of mind. See, sometimes even as Christians we have to be reminded of God's Word. It brings us back to focus. By helping this Christian get back on track, I felt better in body, mind, and spirit, with the added benefit of getting a free dinner out of it.

A few years ago, someone came up with the slogan W.W.J.D. What would Jesus do? A great concept for the time. It helped many people stay calm in their decision-making and brought some peace of mind.

I have a new concept I would like you to take with you. If you choose to use it, that would be great. The next time you are trying to make an important decision, the next time you are trying to decide if you have time to witness to someone, or even help someone, think of what Jesus is going to write down in the, "Lamb's Book of Life."

What will he write down beside your name? Let's you and I make Jesus write down a bunch of positive comments. Let's get Jesus tired of writing gospel things down by our name.

Do you think we can get Jesus to have writer's cramp?

Thank you for your time tonight. God Bless You!

The end of this sermon.

The Challenge of Job

I want you to know that this has been a tremendous privilege for me. I have been transformed over the past two months, through my studies, and the opportunity to share with you my travels through the Bible, and the steps that I have taken in my spiritual quest to come closer to Jesus.

To get the bad news over with first, at least for me, this is my last scheduled testimony tonight. I have to go back to work in a limited capacity, and should be released to full duty as of Friday. Then who know what will happen. My function at my job will be out of my hands. But, I would appreciate the opportunity to speak before you again; unfortunately, it just won't be as regular.

Tonight's message comes from the Book of Job. Now I could talk all night about this story. That is how powerful this story is. To tell you the truth, I have heard the cliché, The Patience of Job; however, I had never read the story until now. Let me tell you, if you have never read this story, you need to get into it. It is a heck of a learning experience.

Job was a very prosperous and righteous man, during his time. He appeared to be very successful, and remember that during this time period, a person's wealth and being was measured by possessions, material things. Job has 7 sons and 3 daughters, 7000 sheep, 3000 camels, 500 yoke of oxen, and 500 donkeys. In today's market, not counting the children, the estimated worth of the animals would be in excess of 4.6 million dollars.

To get into the story...

Now we find that God called a staff meeting with the Sons of God. Angels. Now by reading these scriptures, it shows that God asked Satan where he's been. He doesn't seem to hang out much with the Lord. Satan tells God that he has been walking around the Earth. Then God takes the opportunity to ask Satan what he thought about Job. God states that Job is a blameless and upright man, who fears God and shuns evil. So God is baiting Satan.

Satan then receives permission to mess with Job. However, God tells Satan that he is not allowed to touch his person. This is pretty cool. Satan had to ask permission, and then God warns him not to touch Job's body, and Satan doesn't.

So Job loses all his livestock, he loses all his children, and all that he has left is his wife, I think one servant, and himself. So what did Job do? Did he run around complaining to all of his friends? Does he go out looking for pity from somebody? No, when he lost everything, he simply arose, refusing to blame God as Satan had hoped. Tore his robe, shaved his head, and fell to the ground and worshiped. Saying in his praise, in Chapter 1 verse 21,

"Naked I came from my mother's womb, and naked shall I return there. The Lord gave, and the Lord has taken away; Blessed be the name of the Lord."

In this worshipping, Job never sinned nor charged God wrong. He knew that material possessions in themselves meant nothing in the big picture of life.

Then, God had another Staff meeting, and Satan basically says that the wager is not fair. Nothing has really happened to Job, because it is not his person. Isn't it just like Satan, to complain because he is not getting his way? So God, in proving His point, allows Satan to challenge Job further, but with the only rules of to spare his life.

Now Satan can do anything that he wants, along as Job doesn't die. So Satan places boils on every part of Job's body. These boils were painful, and at one time, the Bible states that Job was scraping the boils with a clay jar part, which meant they were pretty big as well.

Now Satan uses Job's own wife, to challenge Job. Job's wife stated, "Do you still hold fast to your integrity? Curse God and die!

Now that's a great wife to have. One that will support you till the end. No matter how fast you get there. But, Job didn't sin in response to this, he said something to the effect, Are you crazy? Then he stated with a very good question. He asked, "Shall we indeed accept good from God, and shall we not accept adversity?"

Then Job's three friends came to visit, and hung out with Job seven days together without talking about the problem. After all this time, Job finally spoke, and he made the announcement that he deplored his birth. Job shows pain and bitterness about the trials that he is going through. He longed for inner peace. He doesn't curse God during this, but curses his own birth.

Now his three friends have the floor. During this time, his three friends are telling him to repent for whatever the sin is, because only this kind of torment comes to one who has sinned. Now think about the powerful kind of friends that you have. Do you think you could stand daily pressure from people who are suppose to support you, and believe in you, and your beliefs? And then when you need their support, they question your integrity, and ask that you do something that you do not believe in.

But in the face of these three friends, Job turns to God. Job clearly believes that his torment is not because of sin, but has a deeper meaning that only God understands. Job turns to God for answers. Job's presumptuously accuses God of injustice.

In the end, God answers Job and his friends in a whirlwind. He doesn't answer their question, but compares His presence with that of Job's.

Now you want to talk about something getting your attention. God got some attention here. When God got finished with Job, the man who compared himself to "like a prince" who could approach God, Job started to see himself as totally sinful and without the ability to stand before God. When Job came face to face with God he saw that his own self-righteousness, and pride were getting in his way. Job then responds to God in humility. Through this trial and seeing God, Job has now changed from a self righteous, prideful servant of the Lord, to a humble, giving servant from the Lord.

God then vindicates Job in front of his three friends, and turns this into a lesson for Job. God tells Job's friends that they will be basically saved if Job will act as their priest and pray for them.

God tolerates Job's attempt to find out that his problems are from God, but rebukes Job's three friends and their assistance. Job's praying for his friends is a blessing used to heal the friendship between them. Job is able to reconcile with God, and become an even more powerful man of God.

In the end of this story shows us an example that sometimes the difficulties we face are there to make the necessary changes in us that God needs in an effort to use us for what God has in store for us. If we lose our marriage, if we lose our friends, if the money is not coming in like it should, if we aren't being used by God much, if we are injured, God is rebuilding and transforming us into what he needs us to be. Therefore, he can use us to be powerful men and women in Christ.

What else do we learn from this story, what has the example of Job showed us? Satan is defeated. Mortal man can defeat Satan. Glory to God.

Job received restoration with, seven sons and three daughters. And his livestock as before, doubled. His net worth in property is worth an excess of 9 million dollars in today's terms. I read that Job is described as a cross between Bill Gates and Mother Teresa.

In our lives, we have to go through many trials and tribulations, but the Bible tells us we are heirs of God. And joint heirs with Jesus Christ. And if we are to share in the reward at the end of this life, we will probably have to share in the suffering as well. But I guarantee that the pain and suffering we will have to endure here in this life, won't be anything to compare to the glory we will receive when we walk in heaven.

When these trials come in our life, we need to be encouraged by the Story of Job. Remember that when Job went through this, he didn't have a Book of Job for inspiration. God is just letting us know that he believes in us and that we will make it through these trials of this life with God on our side.

Suffering changes you there is no doubt. Suffering happens, you can't stop it. What you can do something about is how you will allow it to change you.

In the end, Satan's challenge and attack is used by God to sharpen and fortify Job's character. While Job appears to be a book about suffering, in the surprise ending it clearly shows it is a book about the sovereignty of God. What Job learns in the midst of his suffering, is a way that no other circumstances could have taught him, in that God is all powerful, all wise, all righteous, and He is good.

Why do the righteous suffer? Because Satan and sin are both real. What good does suffering do?

It strengthens our endurance.

It silences the enemy's accusations.

It gives Glory to God.

It makes us more like Jesus.

It teaches us true dependence.

It purifies our lives.

It rebukes sin.

It enlarges our heart toward others.

So, the next time we are faced with problems in our life, turn to the Book of Job, and compare your problems with what he went through. Find out if they really are as bad as you think they are. When you find your answer, I think that you will find that your problems are not as bad as you thought. When it is put into proper perspective, turn to the Lord, seek Him, and pray to Him for assistance. Your research into Job's trials will put you into the right mindset to praise and worship the Lord.

Thank you for your patience, and God Bless You. I hope that you have enjoyed this journey at least half as much as I have.

The end of this sermon.

If you are reading this portion, then I believe that you have read the sermons that I presented, as a novice, to my church. When you reflect on these powerful words, please apply them to your daily life and see if changes occur for the better in you. I pray that I have been able to pull some of you closer to Jesus, with these works.

God Bless each and every one of you, and praise be to the Lord for guiding us through. Hallelujah!

Author Biography

I am a nineteen-year veteran law enforcement officer with the Henry County Police Department, in McDonough, Georgia. I am married to a beautiful, and caring woman, that is also a police officer. My wife and I have six children with ages ranging from 7 to 19 years of age, and are devout Christians. We attend His Freedom Reigns Ministries, where I give testimonies from time to time through life experiences and what the good Lord provides.

Printed in the United States
200023BV00002B/739-876/A

9 781602 668331